Empath Awakening
How to STOP absorbing stress, pain, and negative energy from others.
Kara Lawrence

Empath Awakening

Kara Lawrence

Published by Kara Lawrence, 2019.

© Copyright 2019 – All rights reserved.

It is not legal to reproduce, duplicate, or transmit any part of this document in either electronic means or in printed format. Recording of this publication is strictly prohibited and any storage of this document is not allowed unless with written permission from the publisher except for the use of brief quotations in a book review.

While every precaution has been taken in the preparation of this book, the publisher assumes no responsibility for errors or omissions, or for damages resulting from the use of the information contained herein.

EMPATH AWAKENING

First edition. September 12, 2019.

Copyright © 2019 Kara Lawrence.

Written by Kara Lawrence.

Table of Contents

EMPATH AWAKENING

Table of Contents

Introduction

Chapter One: Are you empathetic? Understanding these 8 traits that empaths possess

Chapter Two: What Is an Empath? The 9 types of empaths

Chapter Three: What Are Empathic Abilities?

Chapter Four: Why do empaths feel overwhelmed and exhausted? Avoiding negative energy

Chapter Five: Self-healing for empaths

Chapter Six: Empath Awakening: The 3 phases of your empathic growth journey. How to read and use energy.

Chapter Seven: What is Energy Healing and is it Dangerous? Are you an empath healer?

Chapter Eight: Energy shielding for empaths

Chapter Nine: Why are Empaths and Narcissists Drawn to Each Other?

Chapter Ten: Some Pitfalls of Being an Empath

Final Words

Introduction

DO YOU EVER FEEL OVERWHELMED by your emotions or not understand where they come from? Do you ever walk into a crowded room and experience sudden stress for no apparent reason? Do you find yourself completely emotionally exhausted when others share their problems with you, even though they are not your own? Are children and animals drawn to you? Do you sometimes experience mood swings, desire time alone, or have a distaste for violence? Do you have vivid dreams?

This may come as a surprise to you, but the emotions you are experiencing that sometimes seem to manifest from nowhere may actually be coming from the people around you. You may be an empath!

Don't let this thought scare or overwhelm you. There are some amazing and wonderful things you can do with this knowledge, including connecting with the world in a deeper and more meaningful way. You'll be able to understand yourself and those around you better, which is something that may end up changing your life.

Empaths are highly sensitive people who tend to be hypersensitive to the feelings of others and are capable of subconsciously picking up on, "absorbing," and experiencing those feelings themselves. Without the proper knowledge and tools, empaths often become fatigued, overwhelmed, and even frustrated and confused as to why they are feeling the way they are.

With this book in hand, empaths can finally equip themselves with simple techniques for shielding themselves from the negative energy around them and learn how to use their natural abilities for healing.

I spent years of my life not understanding my emotions: mood swings, stress, exhaustion; all for seemingly no reason. It wasn't until I began to understand the empath and highly sensitive personality types that things began to make sense.

Since then, I have learned how to hone my skills and listen to what my body is telling me. There are still days when I get tired, stressed, and overwhelmed, but I can handle them better and stop myself from falling too far into an emotional hole that's hard to climb out of. My mood swings happen less often, and I have better control over my health and emotional well-being.

Armed with the tools provided on the upcoming pages, you too can finally experience freedom from exhaustion, stress, emotional and, in some cases, even physical pain that doesn't belong to you. While you still might have some bad days, they won't feel as overwhelming or as challenging anymore. You'll know how to listen to your body so you can take the time to recharge and set your emotions and mind right. You'll even learn how to discern between your emotions and those you are picking up from other people.

Learn the secrets that thousands of empaths around the globe are uncovering. Proven techniques are here at your fingertips to experiment with and implement on your own for the benefit of yourself and those you wish to share your gift with.

You don't have to hide who you are any longer. Others just like you, who share these amazing gifts and abilities, are no longer staying in the shadows; they are letting themselves be known and sharing their kindness with the world.

They are also coming together to share support and guidance. This is a journey that is incredibly personal, but it's not something you have to face alone. By sharing your thoughts, dreams, and fears with those who are like you, you will get a deeper insight into who you are and discover who you want to be. This book will start you on that journey and arm you with the knowledge you need to help in your self-discovery.

Finally uncover why you may have spent your life experiencing extreme mood swings, being deeply moved and affected by the problems and tragedies of others, and why you require time to "recharge" alone almost daily. Learn that none of these are bad or make you a terrible person. They are part of your healing process, and they shouldn't be ignored or shunned. The only way you can make others healthy and happy is to be healthy and happy yourself.

If you don't have the energy to get yourself out of bed and through your day, how are you going to be there for others? People will ask a lot of you, and you may ask a lot of yourself, but if you don't have the motivation or desire to move, you can't help. You have to help yourself, and this book will give you some ideas on how to best accomplish that task.

Of course, in your journey, you will meet those who may not have the best intentions for your unique gift. They'll be aware that you are special, but they'll try to use that to their advantage. They'll try to break you down, suck away your energy, make you feel like your only job is to serve their needs. This book will help you find ways to combat their attacks.

Leaving yourself disarmed exposes you to the threat of a repeating cycle of toxic relationships, unnecessary discomfort and pain, and your natural abilities falling short of their true potential. Don't spend another day damaging yourself with negative emotion that doesn't belong to you!

The journey to discovering who you are as an empath will be full of ups and downs, joys and sorrows. You will laugh, you will cry, but you will also come out having a better sense of who you are and what you are capable of. With the proper tools in place, you can find ways to help yourself and others without depleting your energy sources or becoming overly stressed, anxious, or depressed. It's worth discovering and honing your skills. You're a kind, caring person, and you should share that with the rest of the world.

The time has come for you to have your own awakening. Understand that the emotions that other people have told you are invalid and that you have been confused about will soon make perfect sense simply by empowering yourself with the knowledge in the upcoming pages. Enjoy!

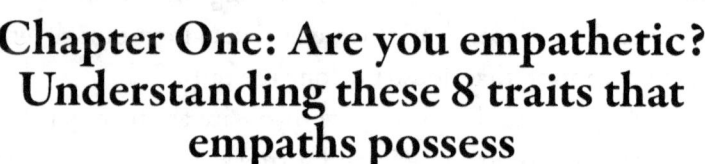

Chapter One: Are you empathetic? Understanding these 8 traits that empaths possess

TO SOME EXTENT, MOST people in the world show signs of empathy (some don't, but we'll talk about those later). This is the ability to put yourself in someone else's shoes and feel the emotions they are feeling. You may not have been through the same experience as them, but with empathy, you can imagine what it feels like.

If you happen to be an empath, you feel these emotions on a much deeper level. In fact, you may feel them before the person you're talking to even expresses that something is wrong or that they have exciting news to tell. It may start as something as simple as a tingling in your stomach, a sense of unease, or the uncontrollable urge to start giggling (and you may actually start giggling). Then, when they start telling you about their problem or joy, everything becomes clear.

Being an empath, you are highly tuned to people's moods. This can be both a blessing and a curse, as you are aware of both positive and negative emotions as they occur around you. But there are many other traits that make you the unique individual that you are. This chapter looks at the other traits that many empaths possess.

Highly Sensitive

For many, the thought of being highly sensitive is viewed as negative. They think that a person who is highly sensitive can't take criticism or gets upset and cries about the most ridiculous things. They may feel like they have to walk on eggshells and police their words so they don't hurt a highly sensitive person's feelings.

This notion that a highly sensitive person is overly emotional is a misnomer. In fact, being highly sensitive means that a person is more in tune with their environment than others. There are some downsides to this, including the fact that a person who is highly sensitive gets spooked easily or can't handle overly loud noises. It also means that crowds and really busy places with lots of colors and activity can overwhelm a highly sensitive person.

They may also cry at commercials or feel sick when they see violence on the news or in TV shows. But this doesn't mean that they aren't in control of their emotions. It just means that they feel their feelings deeply and outside stimuli has an impact on them.

In their own bodies, a highly sensitive person will also be more susceptible to and experience pain on a different level. This means if they get sick or injured, they will feel every moment of agony. If they have their feelings hurt, whether intentional or not, they will feel that incredibly deeply too.

However, most highly sensitive people are aware that they feel and experience the world differently, and they often don't express these things to others. If they are overwhelmed by situations or sounds, they will do what they can to get away. If they are in pain, they often suffer in silence. If a person has hurt their feelings, they may make a comment, but more than likely they will bottle the hurt inside and keep it to themselves.

The only time a highly sensitive person might lash out or react negatively is if they feel trapped. If they are stuck in a crowd or situation where they can't retreat and they are constantly being bombarded with stimuli that they can't control, they will find a way to protect themselves. This usually comes as an emotional release. The intention of this release is not to be hurtful, but a highly sensitive person can't take stimuli like others, and too much can have a major impact on their psyche and well-being.

Enjoy Being Alone

Speaking of alone time, empaths often need time to be alone and retreat after being in stimulating situations. This allows them to recharge and regroup after being flooded with sounds and sights and various emotions.

Most empaths enjoy being alone and don't feel lonely. They enjoy being able to retreat into their minds and think about the experiences that they had and what they learned from them or just veg out and not think at all. In many cases, as an empath, you enjoy complete and utter silence during your downtime. You may curl up with a good book, take a bath, meditate, do some yoga, or just stare out a window—and any of those can make you incredibly happy.

You probably also really enjoy being out in nature, and this is where you can really recharge. Whether it's a walk through a city park, sitting in the backyard, or getting away from the city, you can enjoy the sights, sounds, and smells of nature and the solace that being outside can bring.

More than likely, you are also a huge animal lover. You may even have a few pets at home, and you probably spend a lot of time with them and talk to them on a daily basis. While you're fine with people, you find time with your pets enjoyable because they don't drain your energy or burden you with negative issues. Instead, they fill you with unconditional love and support.

Introverted

Many empaths are introverted. Like being highly sensitive, this is a term that many people misunderstand. They believe that it means you are shy or have social anxiety. While an introvert can be shy and get anxiety about being around others, there's a bit more to the trait than that. Being an introvert means that you are more focused on internal feelings rather than external happenings.

There are introverts who really enjoy being around people, but it can be exhausting interacting with them. This is different for extroverts, who gain energy by interacting with others. As an introvert, you are usually self-aware because you spend a lot of time in your own head dissecting and trying to understand your emotions.

Being an introvert doesn't mean that you don't have friends or enjoy going out. More than likely, you have a small group of friends that you hang out with sometimes. What being an introvert means is that you prefer solitude to loud gatherings and having high-quality friendships over being surrounded by a lot of people.

Ability to Read a Room

Part of your empath abilities allows you to read a room before you walk into it. You feel the vibes, and they probably come over you in waves. If the room is positive and upbeat, you'll probably spend some time hanging out and talking to others. If you get a negative feeling, you will probably leave the situation or—if you can't—withdraw into yourself.

Ability to Read People

As an empath, you have the ability to read people. As mentioned at the beginning of the chapter, you may realize that a person is emotional before they start talking to you. You have the ability to pick up on both positive and negative emotions, and you are often able to tell if someone is lying to you.

This may not be obvious at first, but as you talk to someone, you may feel like something is "off" or that their aura seems dark. You probably get uncomfortable and need to put up a barrier between yourself and this other person, so you may cross your arms and become standoffish. Once you get a chance to get away, you take it and then try to avoid this person as much as you can.

Trust this feeling. Your intuition is letting you know that something isn't right and staying away from them is probably a good idea. Conversely, being around people who make you happy and give you a warm fuzzy feeling can lead to amazing lifelong friendships that you enjoy.

Your ability to read people is often what draws others to you. They feel comfortable and relaxed around you, often allowing them to open up and talk to you about a variety of different things. You may find that this happens with people you just meet and kids. Your ability to make people feel comfortable may lead them to tell you their deepest secrets or unloading emotional baggage. In most cases, you don't mind because as an empath, you have a desire to help others.

A Good Listener

Part of being able to read people means that you are also a good listener, and others can pick up on this readily—which is probably why they start sharing with you even after you've just met. As mentioned, you don't mind when someone does this because you genuinely enjoy helping others and being emotionally connected to them. However, if they start talking about mundane topics, you may find yourself drifting into daydreams or thinking about other things.

As an empath, you want deep connections with people. You want to know all about their hopes, dreams, and fears. It makes you happy and excited to hear what makes other people get out of bed in the morning and what they are passionate about. This allows you to get to know the real them, not the personality they put on in public.

You have the ability to make small talk about the weather if you have to, but it is challenging for you to sustain these conversations for long. When these are the topics of conversation, it doesn't take long for you to get bored and for your mind to drift off. This may also be another time that you withdraw in social situations, finding a place to sit by yourself and not interact with anyone.

Ability to Make Peace

Years ago, I worked in an office that had an open floor plan. For a highly sensitive person, this isn't the ideal work environment because it allows too much stimuli in one area. It also means that every day I sat in a cube with my coworkers and had to find a way to get my work done.

Having people together in this kind of close setting is bound to lead to issues. Someone could walk in after waking up on the wrong side of the bed, or one ehaviour might possess a habit that others find annoying. Maybe they click a pen or tap their foot or slurp their coffee. Something, at some point, is going to drive someone else crazy. As an empath, I am naturally averse to conflict, so I did what I could to ensure that everyone in the cube didn't get on each other's nerves and the day passed peacefully.

After a few years, I decided to move on to another job. When I informed my colleagues of my decision, one of them told me that I couldn't leave because I was the glue that held the group together. That was meant to be endearing, and it spoke volumes about my ability to be a peacemaker and ensure that everyone got along.

Many empaths have this ability. While we know that not all conflicts can be avoided, we do our best to help people see how to handle it like adults and to do as little emotional damage as possible. We don't think that there is any reason for a person to be petty or vengeful, but people are entitled to their feelings. When we see issues arise, we do what we can to diffuse the situation and recognize another's feelings and make sure they are validated and heard.

Creative and Quirky

Being an empath means that you experience the world differently than other people, and that means that you are probably different than your friends and family. You have quirks that make you special and unique. In your younger years, you may have heard from many people that you were "weird," or they'd give you that look where their nose would wrinkle and their upper lip would curl up.

At the time, you probably didn't enjoy being singled out like that. You didn't want to be weird or different, but you also couldn't help it. Now, you should embrace it. Be okay with marching to the beat of your own drum. Your ability to be quirky and different is part of your charm. It makes you stand out from others and go against the status quo. It also gives you the freedom to seek your own path and follow your own dreams.

In addition to being quirky, you probably are incredibly creative. Whether you enjoy creating art, writing, sewing, or cooking, you put your all into your creative endeavors. The only thing more satisfying than creating something is seeing another person enjoy what you've made. This can make your entire day.

The Joys and Sorrows of Being an Empath

If you see yourself in many of these traits, then you are probably an empath. Your ability to read people and your environment allows you to connect with others in deep and meaningful ways. Others view you as a great friend and confidant—even if you are a little different.

Being able to connect with others on this level can be amazing. However, there are some sorrows that come with being an empath. The first is that you are bombarded with emotions all the time—both negative and positive—and this can be draining. The negative emotions are usually the hardest to deal with.

While you are a great confidant for others to talk to, you often feel like they don't give you the same courtesy. They are more than happy to share everything with you, but when you want to talk, they seem distant, uninterested, or just don't listen. When you don't have an outlet for your emotions, they can become overwhelming. Often, this makes you withdraw and isolate yourself from other people.

Thankfully, there are some tips and tricks you can employ to help with this issue, and these are covered in chapters 4 and 5 of this book. The most important thing to keep in mind as an empath is that you are connected to the world in ways that others can only hope to be. They may view you as weird and wonderful—and you are amazing—and that's evidenced by the fact that people want to hang out with you.

Chapter Summary

- Empaths experience the world and others on a deeper emotional level.

- There are 8 traits that most empaths possess, and this makes them unique and special.

- Being sensitive to other's emotions has both positive and negative impacts.

IN THE NEXT CHAPTER, you will learn about the different types of empaths.

Chapter Two: What Is an Empath? The 9 types of empaths

IN CHAPTER ONE, WE looked at the traits that many empaths possess. This should have given you an idea of why you have the ability to interact with others and why you act the way you act. As an empath, you also have the ability to interact with the world in a unique way, often intuitively, and this creates deeper meaning and connections.

Your ability to pick up on people's emotional states isn't something you went out of your way to train for. It's something that happens naturally, and you probably noticed that you've had this ability since you were a child. When on the playground hanging out with your friends, you just seemed to know when one of them was upset or hiding from the others. More than likely, you sought them out and sat with them until recess was over.

As you grew older, this concern and desire to be there for others didn't stop. No matter where you went, you could sense the emotional states of those around you. Of course, the best part is when they are happy and excited because you get to be happy and excited, but you also helped them through the tough times. Both of these can be incredibly exhausting and draining, but it's not something you can switch off.

Being an empath is amazing. However, since every person is different, every empath is different, and you will have different skills and abilities than other empaths you meet. (Yes, there's a chance you will meet another empath.) This chapter looks at some different types of empaths and may help you figure out which one you are.

Emotional Empath

This is one of the most common types of empaths. If you are an emotional empath, you have the ability to pick up on the emotions of others, and you will feel those emotions in your own body. That means if you're around someone who is incredibly sad, you will also feel incredibly sad. The same is true for extreme happiness and anger and all other emotions.

The challenge with being an emotional empath is being able to tell if the emotions you feel are yours or someone else's. Being able to separate your emotions from the world's allows you to distance yourself from the other person and be able to help them without draining all of your energy.

While it's nice to be able to relate to others on an emotional level and put yourself in their shoes, this can take a toll on your emotional well-being. If you really want to be happy about an accomplishment but find yourself being pulled down by a friend who is going through a tough time, your individuality and emotions get lost.

Being an emotional empath creates deep and meaningful connections with others, but it also takes away your self. Feeling another person's emotions and then separating yourself from them is how you maintain your self-identity and don't become enmeshed with everyone you meet. It can be challenging, and it doesn't make you less of an empath and you can still be a good and helpful person, but it gives you your energy and your individuality.

Intuitive/Claircognizant Empath

If you are an intuitive/claircognizant empath, you have the ability to read people just by looking at them. Some describe this as being able to see a person's energy or read their aura. No matter how you describe it, having this skill immediately lets you know if someone is happy, upset, or lying to you.

You may even have clairvoyant or precognitive dreams or feelings. You may experience a sense of déjà vu and just know that something is about to happen. It may not always be possible to pinpoint exactly what is going to happen or change the situation, but having some forewarning may help you prepare for whatever may come your way.

If you are this type of empath, you generally surround yourself with people that have good energy or auras. You will avoid people who make you uncomfortable or who don't "feel right." Since you can pick up on people's intentions and emotions just by looking at them, this can make being in unfamiliar groups or around strangers challenging. Finding a way to shut out the energy and auras can give you back your energy.

Physical Empath

As this type of empath, you have the ability to sense illness and physical discomfort in others. You may feel this as a pain in your own body or just know that something is wrong. Many people who have this ability will go into some type of healing field, as this gives them the chance to help others and get them on the road to recovery.

Intellectual Empath

If you fall into this category, you have the ability to communicate with others using different jargon and vocabulary. This doesn't mean that you will instantly start talking a foreign language, but you will be able to pick up on slang or idioms a person is using easily and readily. In most cases, you will not have been exposed to the terms before, but you have the ability to read the other's ehaviour and pick up on their meaning.

This makes you a social chameleon, able to fit in with many different groups and people. Some may classify you as a social butterfly because you can move easily from one group to another and get along and understand what each one is talking about. This makes you incredibly endearing and charming because you can act as a bridge to bring others together and you have a wide range of people you enjoy interacting with.

In chapter one, it was mentioned that most empaths don't enjoy making small talk. If you are an intellectual empath, you can engage in many conversations with an array of interesting people that is both stimulating and exciting. With this ability, you might not ever have to engage in small talk again!

Geomantic Empath

If you have this ability, you are attuned to the physical landscape. This gives you a deep connection to specific places—often for no apparent reason. Other places may make you feel uncomfortable, and you may not understand why. You are often deeply connected to the natural world and feel sadness or grieve when it gets damaged.

As this type of empath, to do what's best for the world, you may take up environmental advocacy and enjoy spending time in nature. You are probably incredibly comfortable sitting by yourself next to a stream or hiking through the woods. You find comfort and solace away from others, letting the natural world surround you. When it comes to your home, it is probably filled with plants, and you probably prefer natural smells and fabrics to man-made ones.

Plant Empath

If you find that you have a natural ability to grow gardens or plants in your home because you just seem to know what the plants need, you are probably a plant empath. This may have also had an impact on the job you've chosen, and you probably work with plants in some shape or form.

For some people who fall into this category, they claim that they get guidance from the surrounding plants, with the information being directed into their mind. As a plant empath, you probably structure your day and your life so you can have a lot of contact with plants and trees and spend a lot of time hanging out in nature.

Animal Empath

Like a plant empath, if you are an animal empath, you just seem to know what animals need. They are probably drawn to you, too. As a kid, you may have been the one who always found the stray or injured animal and brought it home to take care of it. The older you got the more focused you became on animals and you may currently work in a job where you can take care of them.

If you are an animal empath, you may prefer the company of animals over being around humans, and you may also be vegan so that an animal never has to suffer because of your actions. Some animal empaths report being able to communicate telepathically with animals and say that is how they know exactly what the animals want and need.

Telepathic Empath

If you seem to know what another person is thinking, then you might be a telepathic empath. Being able to read another person's unexpressed thoughts can be both a good and bad thing. It can help you connect with them on a different level, but it can also be disconcerting to know exactly how they feel about you or others. This can also become overwhelming and stressful if you are constantly bombarded by people's thoughts. Finding a way to block them out can help your emotional state and keep you from becoming stressed.

As a telepathic empath, you might find yourself randomly thinking about a person and then they call you or you have an overwhelming need to get in touch with them. This could be because you are picking up on their thoughts of joy or distress. Even if you haven't talked to that person for years, you will have a need to get in touch with them and find out what's going on.

Spiritual Empath

This is often referred to as a medium or even a physic. If you possess this ability, you can connect with spirits or people in other realms. This could include people who have died or beings that exist within your belief system—including angels, demons, tricksters, or whatever.

In your communications, these beings might give you information about the future, past, or just want to talk. They can help you form a deeper connection with the physical world and the spiritual realm that exists beyond. It can be a great way to get a deeper insight into yourself and the people around you.

What Type of Empath Are You?

With the different types of empaths that exist in the world, you may find that you have more traits in one category than another. However, it may also be possible to fall into more than one category. You may be an emotional and spiritual empath or a telepathic and physical empath. You might also be really good about knowing what both plants *and* animals need.

The amazing thing about empathic abilities is how you interact with the world. You just have this sense about people and places, and you have this ability without any formal training. Your abilities have probably always been there. Despite the fact that you didn't learn these traits, and they just showed up, you can still hone them and make them stronger.

This is something that will be discussed later in this book. Being in tune with your gifts and abilities will allow you to keep your thoughts and emotions separate from others and prevent you from getting drained or bombarded from negative impacts. It will also allow you to listen more closely and be better able to help people and the world.

Chapter Summary

- There are 9 different types of empaths, and each one has a unique and special ability.

- Empaths aren't taught their special skills, they are just abilities that exist.

- It's possible to have one or more empath traits.

IN THE NEXT CHAPTER, you will learn about empathic abilities.

Chapter Three: What Are Empathic Abilities?

WE'VE LOOKED AT TRAITS and types of empaths, and by now you may be getting a sense of what type of empath you might be. Remember, it's possible to possess more than one trait and be able to experience and interact with the world in more than one way. In reality, you may find that you have various abilities in all the empath types—and that's okay. You have the option to develop one of these gifts more than others or find a way to make all the traits work well for you.

Being an empath *is* an exceptional gift, but it's not really understood how and where it comes from. There have been attempts to determine how an empath is able to process information around them and feel the emotions of others, but no one has come up with a concrete explanation. It's also unclear how you might get this trait, whether it's genetic or learned. Many believe that it's genetic, as parents who claim to have some psychic or empathic abilities also have kids who possess these traits.

Empathic Abilities

When it comes to empathic abilities, this is the ability to feel what another person feels. You can sense or know that something is up often before they say anything. This could be due to how you read their energy or aura or by tapping into their thoughts. No matter how you get the data, many believe that they get information in some mystical or divine way.

You gather both positive and negative data from the world around you. You can be a human lie detector and know which people to avoid because they are untruthful or manipulative. Conversely, you also know who are true friends and really good people because you can sense it deep within them.

This allows you to connect to and perceive your environment in ways that others can't. You may also have what you call your "inner voice," and this is often where information about the world comes from. More than likely, you hear this voice in your head. For some, though, it may sound like it's being whispered by an outside source.

As a child, I distinctly remember always having this voice or awareness, but it didn't become fine-tuned until I was older. My empath trait is intuitive or precognitive, and I can remember as early as grade school that I would love to go to bed and dream because that reality seemed truer than the real world. I would get messages and information in my dreams, and it would allow me to navigate and get through my day.

As you can imagine, this information was straightforward and easy to understand. In many ways, it was cryptic and could be slightly confusing. However, as I honed my skills and learned how to interpret my dreams, they made more sense. Of course, dreams and precognitions can't always give you the full story, so sometimes you just have a *feeling* that something is going to happen, but you may not know what.

When I was young, since I had no other way to explain my inner voice to people, I just told them it was my guardian angel. Since I seemed to know things about others—sometimes before they knew it themselves—I was looked at with a discerning eye. Since I didn't want to be weird or an outcast, telling them I had an angel seemed to be a sufficient answer. It stopped the weird looks and let me know that I wasn't actually crazy.

With the passage of time, I didn't lose my empath abilities, but I didn't put as much faith in them. Life has a way of beating you down and making things challenging, so even though the voice continued to talk, I ignored it or I drowned it out with alcohol. Due to outside challenges and issues, I stopped trusting my gut instincts and started listening to other people. This led to the development of a lot of issues.

The Downside of Being an Empath

Having the ability to take on other people's emotions gives us the unique ability to help them—and we usually want to help others. As empaths, we are kind, caring individuals who want to see everyone get along and want the world to be a beautiful and inspiring place. However, others don't see the world the same way we do. As I'm sure you've discovered, there are people in this world who are only out for themselves and will do whatever they can to get what they want.

Because of an empath's kind and caring nature, we take on the role of a fixer. We want to make others better people and do what we can to make them happy. We'll take on their problems and offer them advice. We may even do things such as babysitting their kids, clean their house, or take on other errands because we think that's what they need to feel better and be happy.

In many ways, we want to make people like us. We want them to be as loving and caring and emotionally bonded to the world as we are. Empaths believe that if we can show others how amazing this world is and how beneficial it can be to be connected, then everything will get better. Wars will stop. Hate will go away. Love will take over.

This may seem like a rose-colored way to look at the world, but take an honest look at yourself and what you do. When you are being kind and truly helping someone, it feels good. More often than not, they are appreciative, and may even be happy for a while. If they could pay that forward, life would be amazing. Unfortunately, not everyone has our abilities or views. This can lead to being taken advantage of.

There are people in the world who use others to feel better about themselves, and this topic will be discussed further in chapter 9 when discussing narcissists. However, they aren't the only people who will take advantage of you. Anyone who thinks they can get a free emotional ride at the expense of another will take it if they can. After you fix their issues, they will then disappear from your life. This, as you can imagine, is where our fears of abandonment and rejection come from.

In addition, with our actions focused outward, we will often forget to take care of ourselves. This means that we can easily fall into depression and anxiety. As highly sensitive people, we can also get our feelings hurt easily by others. When this happens, we may find that we withdraw into ourselves and feel lonely and even abandoned.

Inability to Change

While researching this book, I came across a video that talked about the ten things that empaths have a hard time with, and one was change. My initial reaction was to dismiss that observation; empaths have the ability to change to fit into all kinds of situations so they can be there for those who are hurting.

As the video continued, it explained that the inability to change has to do with our caring natures and ability to absorb the emotions of others around us. We can't change that part of who we are. In some cases, we can't even shut it off. No matter how many drinks we have to dull the sensation or other coping mechanisms we might turn to stop feeling, *we can't stop feeling*.

That made more sense to me. It's not something that we can shut off. I've attempted to in the past, and maybe you have too. When I did, it felt like a part of me was missing, like I was no longer whole. That was tough to deal with as well.

The inability to change is also coupled with another empath trait that many of us possess. Many of us have a hard time opening up to other people. We are more than happy to help anyone through difficulties they may be experiencing, but when it comes to our problems, we don't know how to ask for help—and we hate to talk about ourselves or be the center of attention.

This could actually stem from a lot of different places, including hurt feelings, fears of abandonment, and feelings of isolation. Throughout much of my history as an empath, I had people come and go throughout my life, many who were just looking for a quick pick-me-up—which I was more than happy to supply—and then they were gone.

Being abandoned in the past makes it hard to trust that others will give us the same courtesy when it comes to our emotions and issues as we give to them. The world has shown us over and over that it's cruel and people are only looking out for themselves. That doesn't change how we approach others, but it has a major impact on how we let people approach us.

Taking on the World

Empaths are often considered rare, fantastical gifts. We are the world's unicorns. We have an uncanny and unexplainable ability to pick up on other people's emotions and have a deep and meaningful connection to the world and the plants and animals that live in it. We know things, even if we don't know how we know things. This is both a blessing and a curse.

While there are a few people in this world who appreciate and love empaths for who they are, we often feel lonely and isolated. In some cases, we may even try to deny our abilities just so we can fit in and not be viewed as different.

The world can be a cruel and challenging place. What an empath brings is awareness and another way to view the world. While an empath gets drained easily of energy when helping others, we still see the beauty in the world. We know the value of being connected and kind. We may weep for humanity, but we also want to find a way to save it.

Chapter Summary

- Empaths have the ability to feel the emotions of others.

- Empaths want to help others live better, happier lives.

- It can be challenging to be an empath, and we may experience depression and anxiety.

IN THE NEXT CHAPTER, you will learn why empaths feel overwhelmed and exhausted.

Chapter Four: Why do empaths feel overwhelmed and exhausted? Avoiding negative energy

AS YOU CONTINUE ON this journey of discovering who you are as an empath, you will become aware of how amazing you are. You aren't the only one who sees this; there are others in the world who recognize that you are something special. However, not all of them want to celebrate your gifts, they may want to exploit them.

Absorbing and feeling the emotions of the world can be incredibly exhausting. From the moment you leave your house, you are being bombarded by everyone else's emotions and energy. This happens while commuting to work, at work, with your kids and your spouse, when you spend time with extended family and friends. The only time you get a break from this onslaught is when you are alone.

While not all the energy that you are hit with is negative, a lot of it can be. In many cases, negative energy is more demanding and louder than positive, so it may be what you pick up on whether you want to or not. Plus, people who are looking to exploit you don't often have good intentions, so you will be exposed to their negativity as well. These individuals are referred to as energy vampires. Unlike vampires who drain you by drinking your blood, these people take your energy away by demanding nonstop attention.

What is an Energy Vampire?

Energy vampires can be anyone, from friends and family to coworkers or strangers you meet in the street. They feed off your emotional energy to give themselves a boost. In most cases, an energy vampire will lack empathy, emotional maturity, and sensitivity. This usually stems from insecurity or inner pain. Thus, to make themselves feel better, they prey on the vitality and happiness of others.

As an empath, you have a desire to help others, and energy vampires will seek you out because they think you can solve their problems. Without healthy boundaries (and perhaps not realizing the person is an energy vampire), you will let them in and try to help. This, as you can imagine, will end up costing you. An energy vampire will drain you to the point where you are no longer able to take care of yourself.

It's easy to look at energy vampires with a scornful eye and believe they are terrible people. But it's important to recognize that they are people who are in pain, and they don't have the emotional maturity or self-awareness to deal with it in a healthy way. This *does not* mean it's your job to fix them. Only they can fix themselves.

When it comes to recognizing whether a person is an energy vampire, there are some things you'll need to look out for. Keep in mind that like people, energy vampires will be different and fall on a spectrum. Some may not be as bad as others, and there are those who will be the worst of the worst.

Being an energy vampire isn't a clinical diagnosis. In fact, the term is more slang than professional. People who exhibit these traits may or may not have a mental disorder, such as being a psycho- or sociopath, a narcissist, or have a borderline personality disorder, but some might. In some cases, being an energy vampire could be a learned trait. As mentioned, there are different types of energy vampires, so be on the lookout for them.

Victim Vampire

For this type of energy vampire, they will present themselves as being at the mercy of the world. Someone or something is always out to get them, which is why they can't seem to get ahead or catch a break. They will refuse to take responsibility for their own actions and may even try to make you feel guilty for not helping them.

More often than not, this type of vampire suffers from low self-esteem, and they don't feel like they receive enough approval, appreciation, or love. This is what they will expect you to give them, and if you don't do it to the degree they desire, they make you feel guilty so they can get more from you to feed their need.

Dependent Vampire

This person probably has really low self-esteem and fears doing something wrong. They will constantly ask questions and need detailed instructions on how to solve their issues or do their job. They may have good intentions, but constantly trying to reassure this person and help them with simple tasks will take up a lot of your time and drain your energy.

Dominator Vampire

This energy vampire always needs to feel superior. Their insecurities revolve around being wrong or weak, so they overcompensate by being intimidating and loud. They will have rigid beliefs and see the world in black and white. Any opinions or views that differ from theirs are wrong, and they aren't shy about telling you why. It doesn't matter if they are flat out wrong, they will express their thoughts and ideas and no one can tell them anything different.

These people are more than likely bigoted, racist, and sexist. They will try to scare you into thinking they are right. They need your energy to continue to feel larger than life and validated in their opinions.

Narcissist Vampire

We will dive more deeply into empaths and narcissist in chapter 9, but I wanted to mention them briefly here because they are absolutely an energy vampire. If you have to deal with a narcissist, you are dealing with a person who has no ability to show empathy or even care about people. They view others as objects, a means to an end, and they will do what they can to get what they want. In their minds, the world revolves around them, and everyone should serve their needs and do exactly what they say. As you can imagine, this can quickly drain any energy you might have when trying to help this type of energy vampire.

Egomaniac Vampire

This type of vampire thinks that they can take up all of your time because their needs and desires supersede all. This could be a subset of a narcissist vampire, as they often feel entitled and that the world owes them something. They will also make it a point to drop names of famous or successful people they know and minimize or ignore the work of others. In some cases, they may even say that you are too sensitive or overly dramatic when you try to help them.

Judgmental Vampire

This person will have an incredibly low sense of self-worth, and the way they talk to you is more than likely the way they talk to themselves. They will focus on your insecurities and make themselves feel bigger by making you feel small. They will do this through shame and other manipulative tactics to make you feel like less of a person.

Melodramatic Vampire

We all know those people who thrive on drama. They always seem to find themselves enmeshed in one issue or another. If a crisis doesn't present itself, they will create one. There are many reasons why a person might do this. Some may want to play the victim of some perceived wrong or may want to be the hero by working through the issue. They may also thrive on other people's anger.

Melodramatic vampires often have an emptiness in their lives, and the only way they think they can fill it is through drama. You are probably aware that constant drama is incredibly exhausting, and this vampire will use it to drain you emotionally.

How to Effectively Isolate Yourself in a Healthy Way

As mentioned, people who are energy vampires will fall onto a spectrum. Some will be incredibly overbearing and hard to deal with, while others are more subtle in their approach. It's important to realize that they may not come out and overtly reveal they are an energy vampire. More often than not, they will be manipulative and crafty about how they suck away your energy. They know that if they are overbearing, they will push you away and not get what they need.

In addition, it's possible for a person to have more than one energy vampire trait. You may find a person who is both a victim and melodramatic. Someone could be dependent and an egomaniac. The most important thing to remember is that they suffer from deep-seated issues. They are often hurt individuals who are looking for reassurance and validation. However, their approach to finding those aren't healthy. They expect *you* to fix them, which isn't something you can actually do. They have to fix themselves, but many of them aren't willing to do that.

The only way to keep an energy vampire from draining you is to isolate yourself or create boundaries. This can be challenging, especially if you don't realize that you are being drained and manipulated.

Recognize your role

People can't take your energy from you. It's not like a blood-sucking vampire that holds you down and pulls the blood from your body. You will play a role in the process. Whether you are meeting them for coffee or indulging them in conversation, that gives them permission to take your energy.

Form boundaries

You have the option of deciding when and how you want to engage with an energy vampire. If it is a close friend or family member, cutting them completely out of your life can be challenging—and may not be an option. However, to ensure that you have the ability to take care of yourself and you aren't left constantly feeling tired and spent, you need to create some boundaries.

What these are will depend on the type of energy vampire you are dealing with and your personal preferences. You may be more than happy to listen to the person talk about their problems, but you may limit them to an hour. Afterward, *you* have to enforce the boundary. The energy vampire will do all they can to get you to stay, but you must remain firm and get out of the conversation.

If you are dealing with vampires who belittle, undermine, or make you feel guilty, let them know that you will not listen to them or deal with them if they are going to be disrespectful. They will test this boundary, and when they talk to you in a demeaning or disrespectful manner, stay true to your word and end the conversation. This may require you getting up and actually leaving or focusing your attention on another task.

Reduce or refuse contact

In addition to creating boundaries, you may find that you will have to reduce or completely refuse contact with an energy vampire. This could apply to both family and friends or even coworkers. Only you can decide what is best for your wellbeing but stick to your guns. Again, they will try to get back into your life to take your energy, but you have to stop that from happening. Eventually, they may get tired of trying and move on to find someone who is easier to exploit and drain.

Be kind to yourself

As an empath, you want to be able to help other people, and these people are reaching out and do have serious problems. However, you can't fix them. No matter what you do, it will never be enough and they will constantly need more and suck more of your energy away.

You can't change your desire to be kind or to feel the emotions of those around you, and these energy vampires know that. They will exploit that and use it to their advantage. Whether you realize what they are doing right away or it takes a while (maybe even years) before you realize what happened, don't be too hard on yourself. You will also slip up every once in a while and get sucked back into their game. When this happens, don't get mad at yourself.

Just like you are *really good* at being there for other people and wanting to help, energy vampires are *really good* at sucking energy and getting others to give in to them. They can be incredibly deceitful and manipulative, and they know exactly how to play on your sentimentalities. Staying strong, forgiving your transgressions, and reassessing boundaries will help you get back on track.

Is My Empathy Draining My Energy?

Chances are, if you are dealing with energy vampires without healthy boundaries and feel emotionally and physically exhausted at the end of the day, your empathy is draining your energy. There are some other signs that you might also be suffering from empath compassion fatigue.

You are emotionally and mentally exhausted

There is a difference between being tired after a long day and being emotionally and mentally exhausted. Emotional and mental exhaustion are often associated with stress, which can certainly rise when dealing with an energy vampire. You may also experience feelings of hopelessness, irrational anger, a sense of dread, nervousness, and difficulty concentrating, among other symptoms.

Despite your exhaustion, you won't be able to fall asleep or if you do, you won't be able to stay asleep. Your mind will race with uncontrollable thoughts, including those that pertain to other people and how you interacted with them. You may develop anxiety and find that you are becoming more cynical and pessimistic.

You dread seeing people

This goes beyond your normal need to isolate yourself to recharge and may get to the point where you don't want to interact with close friends or family (including your children) for fear that they will need something from you. You are so tired that you honestly don't think that you can even give them 5 minutes of conversation because it will take too much effort.

Your dread of seeing people may mean that you intentionally isolate yourself so you don't have to deal with anyone. This may mean calling in sick for work or playing sick at home so you don't have to talk to anyone. You may cancel plans to meet with friends or family or refuse to answer their emails, calls, or texts.

Your compassion and empathy are replaced with numbness

When an empath experiences fatigue, they may no longer be in touch with the one trait that makes them so special. They are tired of being there for others and so exhausted from helping them that they essentially shut down. While it may be nice for a while not to feel anything, if this continues for an extended period, it will become uncomfortable and disconcerting.

Being disconnected is not who you are. Being numb and unable to feel the world and others is not how you get through the day. While these sensations can be overwhelming, you need them to know that you are alive and part of something bigger than yourself. Feeling numb for too long will lead to other issues, including depression.

Do What's Best for You

Unfortunately, you won't be able to avoid energy vampires unless you cut yourself completely off from the world. However, you know as well as I do that this isn't an option. To ensure that they aren't taking too much of your energy, stay in tune with how you're feeling and create healthy boundaries. As an empath, you have a desire to take care of other people, but you can only do that if you take care of yourself.

Chapter Summary

- People will exploit your desire to help others and drain your energy.

- While it's easy to view energy vampires as monsters, they are actually people who are hurting.

- You have to take care of yourself before you can take care of others.

IN THE NEXT CHAPTER, you will learn how to self heal.

Chapter Five: Self-healing for empaths

IN THE LAST CHAPTER, we talked about some reasons why you might feel exhausted and overwhelmed and how to create boundaries to reduce the negativity and feel better. In this chapter, I would like to focus a little more on the healing aspect of being an empath.

We've talked extensively about how empaths feel the energy and emotions from people and the world around them. In many ways, this is sensed as a vibration. Some days we can feel them coming over us in waves, while others it is a buzz surrounding us. No matter what type of vibration we feel, they have an impact. We want to be able to help those around us, but it's also exhausting to do so.

The reality is that every human being has the ability to be an empath. It's a state of being connected, of understanding and being aware of another person's emotional state. Human beings have various emotions, but we all experience them and we all feel something on some level. But because of our upbringing, beliefs, or due to desensitization, a lot of people aren't in tune with their fellow humans. They don't sense their emotions or feel vibrations. They are more than happy to go through life just taking care of themselves.

It's also important to point out that being an empath and having empathy is not the same thing. An empath doesn't have to have empathy to be able to sense emotions, and others can also put themselves in their friend's shoes and understand what they are going through without feeling their emotions. Depending on how you were raised and your own circumstances, you might not be compassionate and caring, but that doesn't stop the wave of emotions from washing over and through you.

Because of an empath's ability to sense and feel all the vibrations in the universe, this usually ends up taking a toll and draining us of our energy. If bad or negative things are happening in the world, we feel that much more deeply than other people. Often, we won't even watch the news because we know there will be something upsetting and negative on it. It's not that we don't care, it's just that we can't do anything to help, and that makes us feel worse. It's also exhausting taking on all that energy.

When it comes to taking care of yourself, you need to practice some self-care techniques before you get to the point of being completely rundown and empty. This is when illness can take over, and that will lay you out longer. Let's look at some ways you can take care of yourself so that the world doesn't drain you of your energy.

Remember How You Function

You have to remember that you are an empath and that you can feel and absorb other people's emotions. Many times, when you get worn out and tired, your desire is to turn away and shield yourself from this. This is fine for a short amount of time and can help you heal, but it's not a long-term solution. Trying to shut off a part of yourself is going to take a lot, leaving you more exhausted than before.

To heal, your goal shouldn't be to resist other people's pain but learn how to open yourself to it, feel it, and then let it go. It's not your job to take on every emotion and try to fix it, but you can recognize that it's there, process it for a moment, and then send it back into the universe. This takes less energy and allows you to be who you are.

It's Not Your Job to Fix Everyone or Take on Their Hurt

When you feel other people's emotions, you often take them into yourself and feel them as if they were your own. This gives you a way to connect with them and help them through their issues, but there's only so much you can do to help others. You can't actually fix their problems for them or take away their emotions. You can empathize and offer advice, but they have to do the work to fix themselves.

Many times, people don't want to fix their problems. They may feel safe in their misery or they may thrive on being a victim. They are more than happy to have you take their energy and exhaustion and try to fix things, but you can't do anything but lend a shoulder to cry on and some advice. To care for yourself, you need to realize that it's not your job to fix others or take on their problems and pain. You can recognize it, process it, and then you need to let it go.

Recognize Your Own Pain

In addition to feeling other people's pain, we also have our own that we have to deal with. This can be incredibly challenging because we often don't feel like we have people we can talk to who will help us through our bad times. We are more than willing to be there for others, but it's hard for us to open up to them. When we are wronged, we also feel this hurt incredibly deeply, so it may be hard for us to trust or let others in.

It's okay to feel pain. It's okay to be unable to help others. Instead of running away from this, we need to recognize it and go into it. If you need to take a moment to break down and cry, take it. This doesn't make you weak, it makes you human. If you have to get angry and scream at the world, then do it. It doesn't make you a failure.

Being able to recognize your own emotions gives you the chance to work through them so that you can feel better. Pain is our body's way of letting us know that something is wrong. If you broke your arm, you would know it because it would hurt—a lot. More than likely, you wouldn't ignore it and you would probably go to the doctor to get it fixed. Your emotional pain is no different. It hurts because your body is telling you that something is wrong. You may not know exactly what it is, but instead of running away from it or ignoring it, sitting with it can be incredibly beneficial.

If this means you need to go to a mental health professional to help with the process, do it. Sometimes getting an outside perspective or just being able to speak your mind freely and openly is all you need to let emotions go. Most psychologists and psychiatrists also have tools and tips they can give you to help you cope with others and the world.

Often when you sit with your pain, this gives you the chance to dig deeper into yourself to figure out what is bothering you. Once you get to the root cause, you can then work on making things better. This is another way of taking in the emotions, sitting with them, and then releasing them.

Separate Your Pain from Others

Part of being able to recognize your own pain is to help you distinguish whether what you feel inside is your own or as the world's. When you are constantly taking on the vibrations and other people's emotions, it can be confusing to know which ones are truly yours and which ones are theirs. That's why sitting with your pain and looking at it to determine if it's yours is so important. If it is, find a way to fix it. If it's not, let it go.

During this process, you need to be aware that you also project feelings and emotions into the world. You aren't just a sponge. When you get to the point of complete and total exhaustion, it's incredibly easy to become a victim and blame the world for what you're feeling and the situation you're currently in. It's easy to tie your happiness or lack thereof to other people.

Just as you can't fix other people, other people can't fix you. At the end of the day, you have to take responsibility for your own emotions and feelings and decide what you are going to do with them. Being able to separate your feelings from others is beneficial for getting you through this and letting them go. That requires being in tune with your pain and happiness and owning what's yours.

Work on Your Self-Confidence

You've been told since grade school that how you feel about yourself will have a huge impact on how you approach life. The more confidence you have, the more risks you're willing to take and the less you care about what others think. They have no power over you because you know your own worth and what you are capable of.

Many empaths fall into people-pleasing (this topic is discussed more in-depth in chapter 10), which means that they need validation and meaning from the people they are helping. They don't feel like they have any value beyond helping others, so they take on this task until they are completely drained and exhausted. They will even change who they are to make other people happy just so they can be accepted, loved, and validated.

You are the only one who can determine your worth. When you are constantly bombarded with emotions and energy from other people and it drains your own, it's incredibly easy to blame how you feel on the outside world. It's easy to get sucked into a "poor me" mentality and let others tell you who you are or who you should be.

It's also easy to think that you are strange or different because of your gift, and others will feed into this as well. When people don't understand something, they have a tendency to look down on it and see it negatively. They won't try to understand you and may even shun and ostracize you. Keep in mind that this speaks more about their personality than it does about yours. Don't let their small-mindedness determine how you feel.

Remember that you have an amazing gift. It can be trying at times, but what you do for other people can be life-changing. Give yourself the same courtesy. Remind yourself that you are capable, strong, and brilliant—because you are. This will give you the ability to handle whatever the world throws at you.

Meditate or Do Yoga

Practicing these techniques is a great way to learn how to clear your mind and be in tune with your body. They can help you understand and focus your energies. They will also give you a way to stay grounded and keep yourself in the moment. Taking time to do this every day is a great way to get in touch with yourself and explore who you are.

When it comes to yoga, this can be a great way to learn more about your chakras and the energy aligned with them. Some believe that if your chakras are out of sync, it will have repercussions on your entire body. Since you are so in tune with and able to absorb other energies, this may be a way to figure out how to work with them and bring them into harmony.

Meditation can help with this and having some knowledge of it is beneficial. In addition, getting some exercise from going to a yoga class is also good for the mind and body and will help alleviate stress. Bringing these elements together can be a great way to help you heal as an empath.

Create a Sacred Space

Having a space that you call your own where you can retreat from the world can help you heal. Where this is and what you do while in the space will depend on personal preferences. Maybe it's your bedroom or your bathtub. Maybe you have a spot in a sunroom or in a walk-in closet. No matter where it is, make sure that it stays sacred. Don't let the outside world in.

While you're in your sacred space, you get to choose what you do with your time. You may want to meditate or do some yoga, or maybe you just want to curl up with a good book or listen to music. How much time you spend in that space will depend on how much time you need to recharge. If you have a family with kids that need to be taken care of, you may not be able to spend as much time in the space as you would like.

However, it's important that when you are in your sacred space, you are fully present. Whether you're there for 5 minutes or 2 hours, don't let anyone encroach on your time. And don't feel guilty about needing your time. You need time away from people to recharge. The better you feel and the healthier you are, the better able you are to take care of and help others.

You Can't Take on the World

Because of your kind and caring nature, you often feel like it's your responsibility to take care of the world. You want to. But you need to keep in mind that you are still a human with limitations and you can't fix everyone. Plus, not everyone wants to be fixed. Do what you can, but remember you also need to take care of yourself.

It may seem odd to need to heal yourself when your gift allows you to heal others, but you are not immune to emotions and bad days. You are allowed to have them, by the way. When they show up, recognize them, process them, and then let them go. Healing isn't always easy, but it's necessary. Since no one else can heal you, it's important that you learn how to heal yourself.

Chapter Summary

- Absorbing the world's energy can be exhausting, so you'll need to learn to self-heal.

- You can't fix other people, and they can't fix you.

- By staying healthy, it gives you the chance to be there for others.

IN THE NEXT CHAPTER, you will learn about your growth as an empath.

Chapter Six: Empath Awakening: The 3 phases of your empathic growth journey. How to read and use energy.

MOST EMPATHS DON'T come into this world aware that they are empaths. They may realize that there is something different about them, but they don't always have the words to explain what that is or what they're feeling. When you are young, this can make it challenging and problematic to interact with your peers. Again, you don't want to be singled out, so you find a way to act "normal." If your abilities are accepted, then you'll likely become more in tune with them.

Sometimes, they are accepted. You may run into family members or friends who have the same abilities as you who encourage you and explain what is going on. If this happens at a young age, it can help shape how you interact with others and set you on a specific life journey. Even if it happens later in life, it can still be an enlightening experience.

When you find out that you are an empath will vary for each person. More often than not, it happens by accident. Either you'll stumble upon your skills and abilities while reading something or someone will point them out to you. You may be young when this happens or you may be well into adulthood. No matter when you find out, there are generally three stages that you'll go through on your empathic journey

Before getting to each stage, it's important to keep in mind that these aren't in a hierarchical order. You don't have to pass through one to get to another and you don't have to reach a certain level to be considered a "true" empath. No matter what stage you are at, own it. It's also important to stay where you are comfortable, so if you like one stage better than another, it's okay to stay there.

It's also important to realize, as mentioned before, that everyone has the ability to be an empath. Some of us are more aware of our abilities, but everyone has the same opportunity to develop and hone their skills. However, if they decide they don't want to, that's their choice. Just like it's your choice to dive deeper into this gift.

With that out of the way, let's discuss the three phases of your empathic journey.

Awareness

As I'm sure you can imagine, the first stage in the journey is becoming aware of your abilities. Again, this is something that can happen early on or later in life and can come in many forms. No matter when it happens, it may feel like a light coming on and everything that you've experienced up until that point suddenly makes sense. This is when you feel like you are experiencing an awakening because you finally have the ability to explain what you've been feeling.

My awakening occurred when I was trying to understand my anxiety. I had been having an incredibly challenging year, with panic attacks and worry pretty much taking over my life. I could barely go a day without feeling an uncomfortable tingling in my stomach or getting dizzy and falling into sheer panic. I was looking for ways to cope with this when I came across an article that talked about empaths and hypersensitivity.

Suddenly, everything became clear. I felt like I was sitting in a dark room with my anxiety and my feelings, but after reading that article, the room was suddenly bright. I realized that a lot of my issues weren't actually *my* issues but emotions I was absorbing from others. Once I had this knowledge, I took it to the next level and started reading and exploring as much as I could about being an empath. Suddenly, it felt like everything about my life made sense.

Empowerment

Once you've had your awakening and are aware that you are an empath, if you're ready, you can take the next step on the journey to empowerment. Some people, after finding out about their abilities or maybe even before, may try to block what they are feeling. It can be overwhelming and tough to absorb so many emotions, and without knowing what to do with them, a person may feel trapped, helpless, and exhausted.

After having an awakening and getting a better understanding of what you can do, the empowerment phase allows you to put your abilities into practice. This is where you'll "play" with your abilities and see what you are truly capable of doing. You may find that you open yourself up to different emotions just to see how they feel. Or you may spend days shutting it off, to see how that makes you feel.

The best part about this stage is being able to take control of your empath abilities. Once you are aware that you have them and what you are capable of doing, you don't have to try to hide from them or shut them out. You can be open and experimental and put yourself out there to see what you are capable of doing to determine how you want to use this amazing ability.

Wholeness

This phase in your empath journey will be taking your abilities and making them part of your life. You don't need to identify or define yourself by what you can do but are aware of what you are capable of. You will move beyond "playing" and just let things just be.

When you're in the empowerment stage, you may spend a lot of time taking on other people's emotions and offering your guidance and advice. Part of this is because you want to help them, but the other part is to validate that your abilities are correct and that you can truly read people.

When you reach the wholeness stage, you will no longer need to do this. You will be confident in your abilities and you will only use them when you need to. No longer will you offer to help others, but you'll wait for them to ask you, and then you'll offer guidance.

Remember, others can sense that you have this skill and ability, and there are certain types of people who will naturally be drawn to you. When you are figuring out who you are, you will be more than willing to offer assistance. When you move into the wholeness phase, you will realize that not everyone can be saved and that you can't take on everyone's problems. When you are whole, you will accept your abilities for what they are, incorporate them into your life, and let them be what they'll be.

Take Your Own Path

Every empath will be at a different phase in their life. Some empaths out there haven't even reached the awareness stage yet. This isn't a competition, so comparing where you are at to others isn't beneficial. In fact, it will probably wind up making you crazy.

Back in chapter two, we talked about the different types of empaths that exist in this world. If you are an emotional empath and you are trying to compare yourself to an animal empath, you've already set yourself up for failure. Don't try to be like another empath, be who you are and focus on growing and expanding your skills.

Again, you also want to be at a place in the process that feels the most comfortable for you. If that means you want to be in the empowerment stage, then stay there. That's your choice. If you want to stay in the awareness phase and not move on, again, that's your choice. You have to do what's best for you and what makes you happy, and that means being able to pick your empath phase.

Reading Energy

Throughout this entire book, we have been talking about how empaths read or absorb energy or emotions. Like everything else, this is something that is experienced differently by each individual. You may take on another person's pain by having an overwhelming sense of sadness and not know why, or you may actually feel physical pain and not realize why.

It was mentioned before that some empaths describe being able to see people's auras, which is the person's energy or feelings that exist around them. Humans let off low levels of energy, and the aura is that energy. Depending on your beliefs, how you view and interpret those colors and energies will vary.

Of course, these aren't the only ways that empaths read energy. It will depend on the type of empath they are and where they get this energy from. Some empaths say the information comes from the spiritual or fourth dimension. If they describe their empathy as telepathic, they may be unconsciously (or perhaps consciously, depending on whether they are aware of their abilities) tapping into a person's thoughts. For others, they say they have the ability to actually see a person's demons.

There may also be cases where the empath is unaware of their abilities, but others sense it in them and are more than willing to open up and share what is going on in their lives. Empaths are generally kind, caring people who are easy to talk to and easy to approach. This may be why you find the stranger on the bus or the kid at the playground telling you their life story. They feel comfortable opening up to you and sharing. You may not have to read their energy at all because they can read yours.

Every person has the ability to be an empath, but only a few will actually proceed down the path and take the journey to help others. There's nothing wrong with this, and everyone has their own place in this world. Don't judge others for not taking the same path as you. You might recommend it and ask if they would like to open up to this ability, but don't force it on them. It is both a blessing and a curse, and only the strongest among us can take on the burden.

Using and Managing Energy

Just because you have the ability to sense and absorb other people's energy, this doesn't mean that you should. Sure, there may be times when it's involuntary and you have no choice, but once you become aware of your abilities, that doesn't mean you have to take on the world. This can be incredibly draining and unwelcome—both for you and the people you are trying to help.

There are many pieces of advice that say you need to shield or protect yourself from the world's energy, and this may be true in some instances, but this can also be draining. It takes a lot of effort to block energy out. The better course of action to take is discussed in chapters three and four, with the key being forming healthy boundaries as well as absorbing, processing, and then letting the energy go.

Don't forget that in addition to being able to absorb energy, you also let it out into the world. If you are feeling negative or down, you are placing this out there for others to feel and absorb. While you are entitled to your feelings and you can't be happy all the time, recognize that the same is true for others. You don't have to take on their emotions, and they don't have to take on yours. Just because they are out there, it's not your job to fix them for other people and it's not another person's job to fix you.

You Can Be Manipulative Too

Don't think that just because you are an empath that you are above the rest of humanity. You are still human, and you will experience a wide range of issues and emotions. While your main goal may be to help others and guide them to feeling better, the opposite can also be true. If you get hurt or upset and feel like others aren't helping you the way you want or need them to, you have the ability to use their emotions and energy against them. You are probably very aware of what will hurt them, and there may be times when you are tempted to lash out.

No one expects you to be a stone or perfect. You can have your emotions and be there for others, but keep in mind that reading people's energy comes with responsibility. Depending on how you use it, you have the chance to be viewed as a hero or villain. Your intentions may be to be a hero, but the other person may view you as the bad guy.

Use Your Power Wisely

Knowing how and when to use your empath power can be challenging. It can also be exhausting trying to fix other people's problems. By focusing on you and being aware of what you need to be healthy and happy, this will help guide you on your empath journey. If you are unsure of whether a person wants your assistance, keep in mind that you can always ask. Making assumptions is what will get you into trouble.

Being an empath is both a blessing and a curse, and depending on the day, you may experience one end of the spectrum over the other. The important thing to remember is that it's a spectrum, so it is possible to find neutral ground. This will vary from empath to empath and knowing yourself and your abilities is the best way to find this middle ground.

Chapter Summary

- Becoming aware that you are an empath is often an enlightening experience.

- You get to decide where you are comfortable in the empath process.

- Everyone will experience this process differently.

IN THE NEXT CHAPTER, you will learn about energy healing.

Chapter Seven: What is Energy Healing and is it Dangerous? Are you an empath healer?

THE ENTIRE UNIVERSE is made up of energy. It's how everything was formed. As humans, we are no different. Our bodies are full of energy. This is often what empaths will pick up on, as well as another person's emotional state. Many believe that to become healthy mentally, physically, and emotionally, the energy has to be healed.

What is Energy Healing?

While the notion of energy healing has only come into practice in the West recently, it has been around for thousands of years. Many ancient civilizations, including those in Egypt, India, the Americas, China, and Japan, practiced this form of healing when illness took hold.

The belief is that people get sick when the energy in the body gets blocked or out of balance. Thus, if it can be freed or realigned and allowed to flow through the body once again, the person will be in balance and feel better. It's believed that a person can heal themselves with energy, or they can visit someone who has the training and advanced knowledge of the practice.

These techniques and practices were once on the fringes of medicine and often referred to as pseudoscientific, but scientists are now changing their perception about energy healing and more studies are being conducted to understand energy and the body, as well as the principles and techniques that are used in energy healing.

Different Types of Energy Healing Methods

There are many types of energy healing methods that are used today, and the goal is to get the body back into balance so it can be healthy.

Acupuncture

You have no doubt heard about acupuncture. This is the practice of placing needles into the skin at certain points of the body to stimulate energy flow. In Chinese medicine, energy highways in the body are referred to as meridians. It is believed that by targeting these meridians with needles and freeing the flow of energy, the person can be relieved of chronic pain and other ailments.

The practice of acupuncture has been in existence for a long time, but it's finding its way into general medicine. In some places, it's part of physical therapy treatments for people who suffer from injuries. These treatments vary from traditional acupuncture because they don't claim to target the meridians. The needles are inserted into specific muscles to create a twitch response, activating the muscle and allowing blood to flow into the area for improved healing.

A twitch response is nothing more than an electrical signal sent from a person's brain to their muscle telling it to move. The thought is that somehow the signal has become blocked, so the needle will open up the communication channel and get the muscles working the way they should. This concept is no different from that of traditional acupuncture. Even though there is a slight difference in how these techniques are described, the goal is the same. Needles are used to free some part of the body, whether it's blocked energy or a tight muscle, so that the person can feel better and heal.

Reiki

For people who practice Reiki, they will use their hands to channel the energy of the universe to heal a person's body. This is sort of like a massage, but the patient is fully clothed and the practitioner may or may not place their hands directly on the body. In some cases, their hands hover over the impacted area.

Knowledge of this practice is passed down from a teacher to a student. However, some colleges and universities in the U.S. are now offering this practice in certain classes and curricula. For those who have experienced this technique, they say that the area where the energy is being directed will become warm or feel like it's vibrating.

The practice was first developed in Japan in the 20th century by Mikao Usui. It was based on the five principles of Meiji, Japan's emperor. These include:

- Don't get angry
- Don't worry
- Be grateful
- Work diligently
- Be kind to others

The practice of Reiki was developed as a way for people to be conscious about their health. It is both a self-healing technique and one that can be applied by a master. Again, the goal is to transfer, balance, and realign the energy in a patient to help them heal.

Qigong

This practice comes from China, and it is a self-healing practice used by individuals to help them get their energy back into balance. While this practice is individual, it can be done in a group setting. It is akin to Tai Chi and yoga. The goal is to cultivate the life force through different body postures, meditation, and breathing. This technique can also develop muscle strength, agility, and balance. Thus, it is used as a foundational practice for many martial arts.

Like acupuncture, this practice targets the meridians and opens up the flow of energy. People who get into this practice are often looking for ways to develop a higher level of awareness, find a higher purpose in life, and reduce anxiety. It is often used in sports medicine, as well as to heal the elderly, as the movements are slow and controlled. Qigong can help a patient develop stability while easing tension.

Reflexology

This practice also comes from China and focuses on balancing the flow of energy, but the target areas in this technique are the feet, hands, and ears. It is believed that different locations on our hands and feet directly connect the meridians to different organs and systems throughout the body. If these can be detoxed and positively influenced, the patient will see improved health.

Massage is used to free up the blocked energy. This is accomplished through stimulation, the encouragement of lymph flow, and muscle relaxation. It is also claimed that reflexology can rid the body of toxins, increase circulation, balance energy, and boost the immune system. The immediate, noticeable effects of the foot massage, such as the feeling of walking on air, is fleeting, but the internal effects of this practice could have a long-lasting impact.

Chakra Healing

In India, chakras are considered primary energy centers. There are seven chakras in our bodies near key endocrine glands and specific areas of our nervous system. In a way, they are like the Chinese meridians, as they form a path from the base of our spine to the top of our heads. When they are functioning properly, energy is allowed to flow steadily throughout the body.

The seven chakras include:

1. Root Chakra, Muladhara – located at the base of the spine at the tailbone
2. Sacral Chakra, Swadhisthana – located 2 inches below the belly button
3. Solar Plexus Chakra, Manipuraka – located 3 inches above the belly button
4. Heart Chakra, Anahata – located at the heart
5. Throat Chakra, Vishuddhi – located at the throat
6. Third Eye, Sahasrara – located in the center of the forehead or the middle of the eyebrows
7. Crown Chakra, Brahmarandra – located at the top of the head

It is believed that the chakras have the ability to open and close, allowing the flow of energy in and out. If there is negative energy, sadness, or anger around, the chakras will close. To open up the chakras to positive and good energy, a person needs to meditate and use certain breathing techniques. This can help bring them back into alignment if they get out of balance.

Crystal Healing

When it comes to energy healing, crystals are probably the first thing that comes to most people's minds. Many have a negative association with it, as it is often seen as something only crazy hippies engage in. It definitely has the pseudoscience vibe to it.

While those who engage in the practice of crystal healing attest that it has awesome power, more research is needed to establish if and how it works. What science has found when it comes to many people and crystals, is the power of the placebo effect. The placebo effect describes a phenomenon from medical studies. People are given something, usually benign pill, and they are told that it will cure their ailments. In some patients, because of the power of their mind, it has the same effect the real drug would have.

Scientists have found the same effect when patients are given crystals. The power of the person's mind allows them to believe that they are receiving healing power, so they feel better. The placebo effect is a real thing, and people can heal themselves or feel better just through positive thinking.

However, those who practice crystal healing, say that it's important to understand that crystals, like everything else in the universe, have energy and carry a specific vibration. Practitioners believe that the color of the crystal lets you know what type of power it contains. These generally correspond to the chakras.

You have the option of using crystal healing on yourself or going to a practitioner to help with the treatment. In most cases, depending on your ailment, stones will be placed on your body to draw out the negative energy or impurities in your body. You also have the option of carrying or wearing charms to promote healing or positive thoughts.

Quantum Healing

The notion of quantum physics and studying the energy in the universe led to energy healing taking hold in the Western world. As we learn more about energy, the impact it makes, and how it is part of everything, we understand how it affects our bodies. The practice of quantum healing focuses on using Life Force Energy of the body to improve a person's health. The technique explores how frequencies impact the body and can give a person the ability to focus, amplify, and direct the energy.

Are Any of These Energy Healing Techniques Dangerous?

When it comes to new techniques and practices that promise to heal your body, spirit, and mind, most people become instantly suspicious. They view it as a "snake oil" or quick fix to problems that only science can truly take care of and correct. They may even claim that these practices are dangerous and can cause harm.

In some cases, it's also claimed that the techniques only treat the symptoms and not the actual cause of the illness. They usually cite things such as cancer or tumors and claim that these can only be healed by medications, which are often dangerous and harmful to the body. This may be true for some people. However, it's important to note that the brain can be an incredibly powerful thing, and with the right type of thinking and techniques, it's possible it can do things we haven't yet seen.

If you've ever suffered from anxiety or depression, you know how much power your brain has over your body. If you have a panic attack, your brain believes that you are in a life-threatening situation and floods your body with various chemicals. Your heart rate increases, your breathing becomes rapid, your throat goes dry, and you begin to sweat. You may even become dizzy. All of this can occur when standing in line at the grocery store waiting to pay for your items. Your brain thinks there's a threat, and your body reacts accordingly.

When it comes to depression, your brain basically shuts you down. You may have a desire to get out of bed and be productive during the day, buy your brain doesn't give you the energy you need. It also messes with your ability to eat, either making you crave things that aren't good for you or getting rid of your appetite altogether.

The point is that your brain can make things miserable for you, and it feels like you have very little control. Why can't it do the same to make you feel better? There are numerous articles and seminars about the power of positive thinking, and there are firsthand accounts of how people's lives changed when they focused on the positive and drove away the negative. Thus, if the brain has the ability to make you feel terrible, it also has the ability to make you feel better.

Your brain is really nothing but a series of electrical impulses, and these messages are sent throughout your body. If you could find a way to control them or put them back into alignment, it's possible that you can heal yourself. The reason that science shuns the idea or claims that it may be dangerous is because they don't have the studies and lab results to back it up yet.

That's not to say that there isn't risk involved with these techniques. If you decide you want to try any of these treatments, you need to make sure you go to someone who has had extensive training. As with anything in life, if you go to someone who hasn't been properly educated or trained, the chance of injury increases—that would be like going to a medical doctor who didn't finish their schooling.

What is an Empath Healer?

An empath healer is a person who has the ability to sense another person's physical discomfort and may even experience it themselves. This may be a chronic issue, a recent injury, or perhaps their energy being out of balance. A healer may be able to make a person feel better through touch or one of the other healing techniques discussed above.

Before going further, it's important to recognize that some people see a distinction between an empath and a spiritual healer. They believe that it's possible to be one or the other or even both. However, just being an empath doesn't automatically make you a healer. This is something that is unique to certain individuals.

It is claimed that a spiritual healer becomes a channel for the flow of healing energy and light. A healer is often an empath, but they might not always be. It is believed that healers share many of the same traits as empaths, but they also have some unique to them. These are listed below.

- Highly sensitive to energy

- Feel others' emotions as your own

- Feel others' ailments or issues as your own

- Intuitive, can easily read others

- Big picture thinker and often think in shades of gray instead of black and white

- May have bouts of existential depression

- Felt or have been an outcast

- Think differently than others

- Easily overwhelmed in crowds and will feel drained when around people for too long

- Struggles with panic and anxiety

- Natural peacemaker

- People turn to you in times of need and may expect you to deal with their emotional baggage

- May have digestive issues, lower back pain, or hold weight around the stomach

- Animals and children are drawn to you

- There is a history of healers in your family, including nurses, doctors, massage therapists, physical therapists, etc.

- Might have chronic pain or an autoimmune disorder

- Sensitive to electromagnetic frequencies (EMF)

- Great listener

- Drawn to the healing professions and helping others feel balanced and whole

- Ability to sense and alter the energy around and within your body

- May have had mystical experiences

Like most empaths, as a healer, you probably didn't come into the world aware of your abilities. You may have stumbled upon your gifts while looking for an answer to another question or someone may have mentioned it in passing. You may have always been aware that you enjoy helping others and may even have gone into a field that allows you to do this, but you may not have had your awakening. Once you have your awakening, you can explore the various paths that will help you hone and heighten your abilities based on the practices and techniques that interest you.

Finding the Right Energy Healing

If you're thinking about going in for an energy treatment or honing your potential healing skills, you might be wondering which one you should choose. When it comes down to it, you'll need to find the one that best suits your personal tastes. If you don't like people touching you or you having to touch them, particularly feet, then reflexology might not be the best option. Reiki might also be pushing it unless you can practice the technique without touching.

It's also important to note that when you spend some time in your sacred space (as discussed in the last chapter), you can practice some self-healing techniques. Remember, these include yoga and meditation. There are many resources available both online and in books to help you find the right technique and path to take.

In many ways, the world is still a mysterious place. While science has found the answers to a lot of questions about the universe and our bodies, there are still things they can't explain or don't understand. Energy healing has been around for thousands of years, and people have reported positive results from the practice. Science is coming around to look more deeply into these techniques, and they may find that there is something to them.

Chapter Summary

- There are many energy healing techniques people use to balance and realign body energy.

- Energy healing is gaining popularity in the West, and science is viewing it as more than just a fad.

- Anything can be dangerous if not done by a trained individual.

IN THE NEXT CHAPTER, you will learn about energy shielding.

Chapter Eight: Energy shielding for empaths

BEING CONSTANTLY BOMBARDED by the energy and emotions of other people gets exhausting, even if those energies are positive. Being unable to distinguish your feelings from those around you can lead to a sense of loss, both of yourself and of control. You need to be able to function on a daily basis, so finding a way to block energies and emotions is the best way to accomplish this task. This is often referred to as shielding.

There are different techniques that you can try to find what works best for you. To figure this out, you'll have to test them out. You may find that depending on the time of day and the situation you're in, one method works better than another. The goal of shielding is self-care. It allows you to stop absorbing negative emotions and stress from others before it takes a toll on your mental well-being and physical health.

These techniques work by reducing the stimulus around you and allowing you to center yourself. When you start to feel exhausted or overwhelmed, that's a good sign that you need to put up some shielding or find another way to protect yourself.

Please keep in mind that these methods don't come from medical science and they may not work for everyone. However, for some, the mind can be an incredibly powerful tool, and by utilizing visualizations, this gives them the confidence boost they need to protect themselves and get through their day. In some cases, such as the Jaguar Protection Meditation, it may be useful to draw strength and energy from another entity to give you confidence and protection as you face your day.

Since it's unknown exactly how empaths take on the world's energies, science has yet to create a way to shield you from this onslaught. Until they come up with something, these techniques may be just what you need to keep your energy and stop feeling so overwhelmed.

Shielding Visualization

People put up walls—both physical and metaphorical—for a good reason: because they are good at keeping things out. If you find that you are being overwhelmed by energy and emotions, then putting up a wall or shield is a great way to protect yourself.

To put up your wall or shield, you'll need to start with taking some long, deep breaths. You'll then want to envision a shield of white or pink light that completely surrounds your body and extends a few inches beyond. Nothing can get through this shield, not stress, toxic thoughts or emotions, nor negative situations. The only things this shield allows in are positivity, light, and happiness. You can use these to feel centered and experience joy.

No matter where you are at, whether you're in a crowd, at work, on a bus, or standing in line at the store, you can use this shield to protect you.

Set Boundaries

The notion of boundaries was discussed earlier in the book when talking about energy vampires, and it's a good technique to help when you are feeling overwhelmed and bombarded with energy and emotions, so we are going to discuss it again.

One of the places where you may feel overwhelmed is at work. This can be caused by the new trend of having open workspaces, which is believed to promote collaboration among coworkers. It can also create a noisy and stressful work environment, especially for empaths. With no way to get away from people, you are constantly exposed to their energy and emotions.

The best way to set boundaries in this environment is to put up physical barriers. If you have the option, this could include cubicle walls. If cubicle walls aren't an option, then putting picture frames or plants in your workspace can also create a physical barrier. You might also consider wearing noise-canceling headphones or earbuds to block out conversations and other sounds. These can also be used when in crowds commuting to and from work to reduce the discomfort you feel from other people's energy and emotions.

This is another form of shielding, but instead of visualizing a wall or shield, you are putting up a physical one. You don't have to make it obvious that you are trying to block others out if you don't want to, but then again, you might. You get to choose how you deal with people and your personal space, so you may even tell people that they can't cross a certain line when they come to talk to you. This, of course, can be handled tactfully so that you don't upset your coworkers and make the office a more uncomfortable place to be. Whatever you decide, it's important to do what is necessary to keep yourself energized and healthy.

Every so often, you might make it a point to take a break and go to a secluded, quiet area in the building or outside of it. This can function much like your sacred space, and you can use the time to do some meditation and clear your mind. If nothing else, the silence should help you find your center and allow you to focus on something positive.

At home, you'll want to ensure that you have a sacred space. Once again, this is an area where you can retreat to that is quiet and allows you to get away from others. You'll need to let family members know that when you are in your sacred space, you are not to be disturbed. You don't have to spend hours there (unless you want to), and if you have small kids, then setting a timer may be helpful in reminding them that they can't bother you until the time is up. For younger kids, you might also explain that you need a time out, as this is a concept they might be able to grasp.

The Jaguar Protection Meditation

There are some circumstances and experiences that may make it feel like negativity is coming at you from all directions and in ways that are too much for your shield. When this occurs, you may use the technique known as calling on the power of the jaguar.

This powerful and beautiful animal is a patient and fierce guard that can keep toxic people and energy away. The technique works by bringing yourself into a calm meditative state. You'll then call on the spirit of the jaguar from your deepest heart. You will ask her to protect you. Feel her presence enter your space and then visualize her patrolling your energy field and keeping negative forces and intruders at bay.

The more you can envision how the jaguar looks and how it moves, the more powerful the protection will become. If negative energy or people get too close, imagine the creature's mighty paws batting it away or her showing her teeth and snarling to push them back. Know that whenever you need her, the jaguar will be there. Thank her for that and be secure in knowing she can keep anything away.

Understand and Define Your Relationship Needs

Humans are social creatures, which means we need to be around others to feel connected and accepted. This is true even for empaths. However, to prevent yourself from becoming overwhelmed and exhausted, you need to understand and define what you need from a relationship, and then communicate that to the people around you.

If you need certain things from your partner or family, such as a 10-minute break when you get home from work to recenter yourself and switch from career mode to family mode, you need to tell them this. Then you need to make sure that they don't bother you during this time. If you want to sleep by yourself or have more sex or whatever, then these are all things you need to figure out and communicate to those closest to you.

These will be incredibly personal needs, so you may need to spend some time thinking about your life and what you want. You also have to realize that those around you may not be able to provide these for you. If that happens, you'll have to determine if the person should stay in your life or if there's a compromise you're willing to make.

This may sound harsh and uncaring, but it's actually the opposite. You are a person too, with needs and wants of your own, and you should be able to have those met so you can be a happy, fulfilled individual. If you are always giving to others, this depletes your energy quickly. If those around you can help out or give back in some way, this will keep your energy levels where they need to be so you can function.

Prevent Empathy Overload

Sometimes, no matter how hard you try, you can't stop absorbing all the energy around you. When this happens, you need to find a way to release it. This can be done by inhaling the scent of lavender or spending time in nature. You'll also want to limit the amount of time you spend with people; set boundaries and time limits and stick to them. This is when your sacred space will become the most important. Doing some meditation or yoga can also be beneficial.

Alternative Approaches

For some empaths, shielding themselves from the world is just as exhausting as taking in the energy and emotions. It's not hard to see why. Maintaining and concentrating on a shield or incorporating the Jaguar Protection Method takes a lot of focus. Thankfully, there are some alternatives that you might consider using.

As with the techniques mentioned above, these may not work for everyone. Again, the best course of action to take is to try them out and see if they work for you. You may also find that one works during certain situations while another doesn't. The most important thing about all the techniques is to use them when they work best to conserve your energy.

Turn the Shield into a Filter

Despite the fact that the shield is a construct of your mind, focusing and maintaining this visualization can be tough. It's just like putting up physical walls: the maintenance involved repairing sections the world keeps knocking over can be ehaviour. Instead of having a strong, impenetrable shield, the better plan might be to have a filter. This way, when benign energies or emotions come toward you, you aren't wasting energy trying to keep them out. You can save your strength for the really nasty things that might come your way.

The nice thing about this approach is that you still have some awareness of what's going on around you and you're not completely shut off. More than likely, you don't want to be cut off from those around you. If they are being negative, then you can distance yourself. Otherwise, allow yourself to be open and experience the world.

There's nothing wrong with experiencing other people's energy. You just have to know when you've hit your limit and stop the onslaught before it exhausts you. The only way you're going to be able to do that is to know where your limits are, and this will require taking in energy and figuring out what you can handle and what you can't. When you need to block it out, you have the skills and techniques to do that.

Learn How to Detach

If you get to the point where even maintaining a filter is challenging, then you may want to try detaching from emotions. This won't make you a terrible person or unable to be there for others, but it will save you some energy let you and focus on the important things.

As mentioned, humans are social creatures, and throughout the day, we have a lot of contact with numerous individuals. Sometimes, those people are near and dear to our hearts, such as our family and friends. Other times, they are strangers or acquaintances we pass on the street or at work. The goal with detachment is to figure out which energy and emotions are worth hanging onto and which aren't.

If you happen to stop at the store on your way to work to grab a coffee and the cashier, whom you've never met before, is in a bad mood, this will probably stick with you for most of the day. You will take on their energy and incorporate it as your own. Why? You don't know this person. You can't fix their problems for them. And you may or may not see them ever again.

Being able to detach yourself from the emotions and energies that matter will save you a lot of energy and stress. It may not be easy, but this is something that you can learn to do over time. You'll need to recognize that the energy was negative and then view it without emotion as something that is separate from you.

If it helps, you might think of the negativity as a car passing on the street or a dark cloud in the sky. These things will always be there, but you don't have to chase after them. You can watch them move by, and then you go on with your day, not giving the car/cloud/energy another thought.

Of course, there will be times when you'll want to engage or take on the energy or emotion, and that will be your choice. You have to decide which ones are worth engaging in and which ones aren't. There's no formula for how to do this. However, if you find that you are getting run down and exhausted, you may need to take a step back and re-evaluate the situation to ensure that you are doing what's best for you and for the person you are trying to help.

Find a Way to Let the Energy Flow

For some empaths, dropping the shield entirely and letting the energy flow through them is the most effective way to handle various situations. For some, this may sound like a terrible idea and they may feel overwhelmed and exhausted just thinking about it. However, you need to remember that every empath is different and has different ways of coping.

Besides, for most empaths when they get overwhelmed and exhausted by the raw energy of the world, it's because they aren't letting it flow. They will often take it in as their own and then hold on to the feelings, turning them over and trying to figure them out. The goal with this technique is to realize that the feeling is there, recognize that it's separate from you, and then let it pass through you.

Instead of thinking about energy as a cloud or a car, think about it as beams of light. Everyone has these beams emanating from them. Sometimes they are bright and cheery, and other times they are dark and looming. The point is that they are translucent. They aren't tangible things, so they can pass through you without causing any harm. If you allow them to get stuck and you absorb the light, that's when you get sapped of your energy and strength.

Just like others, you have light emanating from you. If it helps, you can imagine that light from other people as a separate color. Watch it come into you, swirl around for a moment, and then watch it leave. You may even consciously imagine shooting it out from your fingertips, driving it into the ground if it's negative or shooting it into the sky if it's positive.

Remember Who You Are

Back in chapter five, we talked about self-healing for empaths. In many ways, that can also apply here. Being able to shield yourself or at least control the onslaught of energy and emotion is needed for your well-being. Whatever technique you decide to use is up to you, but it should keep you from getting drained by other people. In addition, it's important to remember who you are.

As an empath, you experience the energy from the world around you on a deep and personal level. This can be a beautiful and amazing thing. However, when you try to deny it or put up too many walls, this can be just as exhausting and debilitating as letting these entities overtake you. Don't deny who you are and what you are capable of. Find a way to make it work to your benefit.

Only you know your body, abilities, and what you can handle. Use this knowledge to find the best way to take care of yourself. If you aren't healthy, you can't function. You may be able to sense the world's problems, but you don't have to fix them all on your own. Take care of yourself. You're worth it.

Chapter Summary

- To preserve your energy, you need to find a way to protect yourself from negative energy.

- If you get run-down, this can lead to illness and poor health.

- There are many methods you can use to protect yourself from negative energy.

ARE YOU ENJOYING THIS book? Please consider leaving it a review! (CLICK HERE to leave a review)

In the next chapter, you will learn about empaths and narcissists.

Chapter Nine: Why are Empaths and Narcissists Drawn to Each Other?

WHEN TALKING ABOUT empaths, it seems impossible to avoid mentioning narcissists as well. The relationship between these two types of people is well-documented and well-known, and there are a lot of discussions about it. I'm not going to dive too deeply into the topic in this book because I have written another book specifically about that subject. However, I think it's important to mention it briefly.

If you wish to continue further and explore an entire book focusing on this subject that many of us are affected by, please refer to the companion piece, "Toxic Magnetism," by myself, Kara Lawrence.

What is a Narcissist?

The term "narcissist" is thrown around a lot in our society, often incorrectly. Many times, we'll apply it to people who take a lot of selfies or talk about themselves. While this can be a sign of self-absorption, narcissism is actually a disorder that is recognized by the medical community. It is referred to as narcissistic personality disorder. Some traits a person with this disorder might have include the following:

- An exaggerated sense of self-importance

- Sense of entitlement

- Require constant and excessive admiration

- Believe they are and want to be recognized as superior

- Fantasize about the beauty, power, brilliance, and success of their perfect mate

There are many other traits associated with this disorder, but these give you an idea of the type of person you may have to deal with as an empath. While the person who is taking selfies and posting them on the internet could in fact be a narcissist, they may also just really enjoy the attention. The only people who can diagnose a person with this disorder are trained, medical professionals.

The thing to remember with narcissists is that even though they portray an air of confidence and grandiosity, they don't actually feel it inside. They usually have incredibly low self-esteem and a negative view of themselves and their abilities. However, they don't want the rest of the world to see this, so they put on a mask and create a false self.

In addition, most narcissists are unable to experience empathy. They can't put themselves in someone else's shoes and experience their emotions. They view people as commodities, only put on this world to serve them and their emotional needs. When a person stops serving their needs and making them feel special, they will drop them and move on.

Empaths Attraction to Narcissists and Vice versa

Narcissism happens on a spectrum. Therefore, there are some really bad narcissists in the world that have every negative trait that defines this type of person, and there are some that don't exhibit as many of the traits. They can also slide up and down the spectrum depending on the circumstances.

The tragic thing about most narcissists is that they are often deeply wounded individuals who experienced some type of trauma in their life. This may have been from abuse as a child. Their narcissism may also have been caused by genetics or issues with the neurobiological connections in their brain. When this happens, they don't have the ability to feel emotions like others because of how their brain is wired.

As an empath, you will pick up on how deeply wounded a narcissist is. You will sense and feel their emotions and their pain, and you will want to fix them. It's who you are. You are a kind, caring individual that wants people to feel good and be happier. This person who just came into your life is a wounded bird in need of healing.

While part of you should feel sorry for and want to help a narcissist, it's also important to realize that you can't help them. A lot of what they do is by choice. They may have a tragic past and some messed up wiring in their brain, but they still make conscious choices, and they choose to exploit and demean you.

You see, one of the things that make narcissists the way they are is that they crave being emotionally connected to people. They want what you have: the ability to feel and sense emotions. But at the same time, being able to do this scares them. They've never been in tune with their emotions or they may have been stunted or not allowed to experience emotion as they were growing.

They view you, an empath, as something amazing yet frightening. They want what you have, but they can't deal with the emotions. They see you as both a savior and as a threat. These binaries and inabilities to cope with how they feel make them decide that they have to destroy you, or at least manipulate you so you will take care of them.

Since they are afraid of their emotions and you are so good at dealing with them, they think that you can take over for them. Because you can sense and absorb emotions, they want you to take theirs and fix them. They want to be numb to the world, while you take on all the troubles and problems that they experience.

As an empath, you may think that you can do this. Remember, you will have moments when you can't distinguish between your emotions and others, and narcissists are more than happy to let you think that the emotions you are feeling are yours and only you can fix them. And you'll try. You will run yourself ragged trying to fix their ailments because you will believe that they belong to you.

The problem with this scenario is that you can't fix the other person. Only they can fix themselves, but they don't want to. And this doesn't stop them from feeling. This leads to major issues and frustrations and may even increase the amount of abuse you receive from the narcissist.

Abuse from Narcissists

Narcissistic abuse comes in many forms, and it usually starts out subtle. They are incredibly good manipulators, and they know just how far to push you before pulling you back in with love and admiration. This can leave you feeling confused and lost. Eventually, you may find that you are dependent on the narcissist to function and find validation.

Like the narcissist, the abuse will be experienced on a spectrum, from emotional to physical, but it is debilitating for the one receiving it. The goal of the narcissist is to have you all to themselves, with your thoughts, energy, and emotions focused solely on them. This is how they feel better about themselves, and each one uses similar tactics to accomplish this goal.

Along with the other companion pieces to this book, I have also written an entire book covering the covert tactics of Narcissists titles, "Invisible Abuse" by myself. If you feel like you would like some more information on narcissistic abuse, please refer to this title as well.

They'll Shrink Your World

The vast majority of narcissists are possessive and controlling. They often fear losing control, and this may stem from traumatic experiences where they didn't have any control at all. Now, they want to control everything so they don't feel helpless. This includes you. Thus, to maintain that control, they will shrink your world. They will isolate you from friends and family. They will get angry if you want to spend time with the people you love, or they may try to guilt-trip you into believing you are neglecting them or your children if you have some with the narcissist.

To avoid their anger and wrath, it's just easier for you to decline invitations to hang out with others to only talk to them on the phone or through texting when the narcissist isn't around. You are a natural pacemaker, so you will take on the task and change your ehaviour to make your partner happy. However, you will not get the same courtesy, and they will hang out or talk to friends and family as often as they like. Their world will stay as large as they deem necessary.

Nothing Is Ever Their Fault

Narcissists have a hard time accepting blame. They think that their situation is always because of other people or because the world is out to get them. You will always do something that they don't like. When they do something you don't like, you will be blamed for making them do it. If you try to point out how hurtful, manipulative, and destructive their ehaviour is, they will turn it around on you. They will say that you take things too personally or are too sensitive. More often than not, if you try to point out that they are being abusive, they will have reasons why *you* are actually the abusive one.

As an empath, you will take these things deeply personally. Since you are unable to distinguish between your feelings and theirs, you will start to question whether or not you are being too sensitive. After all, you *are* a hypersensitive person, so you might think that you are taking it beyond normal bounds. You might also think that your inability to fix their problems is because of your anger or emotional outbursts, so you will wonder if your actions do border on abuse.

They Will Always Win

To narcissists, life is a game, and the point is to get others to admire and validate them. They can change how they accomplish this goal depending on the people they are around. Most people won't even know how they act behind closed doors because they appear so kind and helpful in public. When you try to tell them any differently, they will look like you are crazy.

This is a conscious and intentional deceit that narcissists engage in. The more they can manipulate and control people and their environment, the better they feel about themselves—and they will change, bend, and break the rules so that they always come out looking like the good guy. Don't try to use their tactics against them because they'll change the game and it won't work.

The purpose of doing this is twofold: the first is so that they can always win at the perceived game of life. The second is to keep you off balance. If you constantly have to question and wonder what is going to happen next or how the rules are going to change, you can't focus on anything else. You can't find a way to get out of the relationship or find ways to take care of yourself. You are sucked in and forced to play their twisted and damaging game.

They'll Make You Crazy

The other part of keeping you off balance, in addition to helping them win their game, is to make you crazy. You will constantly question your perceptions and emotions. You will start to doubt yourself, and you will begin to believe that you are truly flawed. The first reaction to this will be to try to fix it, but you can't because the rules are always changing and you aren't allowed to have wants, needs, or emotions of your own.

There are many other ways a narcissist will find to abuse you, including seeking revenge if you reject them and trying to pull you back in so that they can reject and discard you. This is something they are really good at, and they have honed their skills to disarm you and draw you in. You may not realize what has happened until years down the road. By then, you may find that you have developed ehaviourncy.

What Is Codependency?

Codependency, like narcissism, is another term that is often misunderstood. For many, they think that a codependent partner is a person who is incredibly needy and depends on the other person. However, there's much more to this term than just the everyday clinginess that most people envision.

If you believe you are affected by co-dependency, you may want to look into my other book I have devoted entirely to the subject titled, "Am I Codependent?" by myself, Kara Lawrence. I will cover co-dependency briefly here and if you wish to explore further, please refer to the companion book.

People who are in codependent relationships will structure their entire life around making sure the other person is taken care of or happy. In essence, a codependent relationship is when one person needs the other person, and that person needs to be needed. The codependent will sacrifice their self-esteem and sense of self-worth to make sure their partner is taken care of, and this partner is more than happy to take all that the other is willing to give. Often without giving anything or very little in return.

Codependent relationships can occur between romantic partners, coworkers, family members, or friends. More often than not, it also includes emotional or even physical abuse. It is also a ehaviour that can be learned and passed down from one generation to the next.

When it comes to empaths and narcissists, a narcissist needs an empath to take on their emotional baggage so that they don't have to deal with their own thoughts and feelings. However, they aren't the codependent ones. As the empath, you will be broken down and told that you can't live without the narcissist. As with everything else, this will happen subtly and covertly. They may get to a point where they are comfortable telling you that no one else wants you and that you are worthless, but this usually happens once you have been drawn deeply into the relationship.

The other tactics they use, such as the crazy-making, shrinking your world, and having unpredictable and often scary mood swings, is often enough to keep you in line and ensure that you cater to their needs and theirs alone. In some cases, they may even use physical violence to ensure that you are focused solely on them. To keep from rocking the boat or making the narcissist upset, you will completely transform and change your life so that you meet the other person's needs and make them happy. This is often at the expense of your own happiness and health.

There is a difference between dependence and codependence. Dependence happens in a healthy relationship, where two people depend on one another for love and support. There is value for both people when they are together. Codependence is when one person feels worthless unless they are needed and will make sacrifices for the other person who then gets satisfaction from having their every need met. These relationships are often valuable only to one person.

Symptoms of Codependency

There are many symptoms that can tell you if a person is codependent. A few of these are listed below.

- They can't find happiness or satisfaction in life unless they are doing things for the other person.

- They often stay in abusive relationships even when they know their partner's actions are hurtful.

- They will do anything to make the other person happy, even if it costs them in some way.

- They constantly feel anxious about the relationship and need to make the other person happy.

- All of their time and energy is dedicated to making sure their partner gets everything they ask for.

- They feel guilty if they think about their wants and needs. Often, being called "selfish" is the worst thing a codependent person can hear, and they'll do what they can to prove they aren't.

- They may ignore their own values, morals, and conscience to make the other person happy.

Avoiding the Narcissist

The relationships between empaths and narcissists have existed for a long time, and it's something that will continue well into the future—or at least until humanity can evolve into a kinder, more caring society. They both need each other in different ways: the narcissist is looking for a way to not have to feel, and the empath wants to fix the world. They will always seek one another out.

Narcissists won't change. They may alter the personality they show to certain people, but underneath their mask, they are the same messed up person who wants others to validate them and shower them with praise. Empaths are good at taking on energy and emotions, and a narcissist is more than happy to dump all of their issues on them.

It can be hard to avoid narcissists because they are really good at manipulating others. As mentioned, you may not realize you have been lied to until you are deep into the relationship. As an empath, one of your talents is that you can often read people and sense when they are lying. Narcissists can be good about coming across as the victim, but if you sense anything is wrong or your gut is telling you to get away, listen to it. Fight your natural urge to want to fix the other person and leave.

In most cases, the narcissist won't pursue you for long. If they can't get what they need immediately, they will search out another victim. It can be hard once you have been sucked into a relationship with a narcissist, but it's not impossible to get out. You'll need a good support system and well-defined boundaries, but they will eventually grow weary and move on.

Being in a relationship with a narcissist can change you in many ways. It may even make you distrustful and leery of other people. You may feel the desire to withdraw and push away your empathic abilities. If you need to do this for a while to heal, then this is a step you should take. But don't shut yourself off forever. Just because some people will take advantage of you, not everyone will. Use what you learned as a lesson and figure out how to help those who are truly worthy of your gifts.

Chapter Summary

- Empaths and narcissists are naturally drawn to one another because of what they can provide.

- Narcissists are really good manipulators.

- Narcissists will drain an empath's energy and leave them questioning their self-worth.

IN THE NEXT CHAPTER, you will learn about some pitfalls empaths may fall into.

Chapter Ten: Some Pitfalls of Being an Empath

BEING AN EMPATH DOESN'T make you a good or bad person. It just makes you, you. You have the ability to decide which path you want to take and whether you want to use your skills for good or not. Most empaths are incredibly kind and caring people, so they will often take the high road. However, you are still prone to normal human emotions, including anger and jealousy, so you may find yourself falling into some dark places at times.

As an empath, there are also some other pitfalls that you may find yourself falling prey to. While every human being is capable of being an empath and sensing and absorbing others' energies and emotions, the vast majority of them don't hone these skills. That's okay. That's their choice. Just like it's your choice to take your empath abilities to the next level.

However, when you do this, you will probably find that this choice makes you different from most of society. Since you are likely already more sensitive, this can lead to some issues. The biggest of which is the desire to fit in. This may lead to you become a people pleaser.

What Is a People Pleaser?

On the surface, it seems like this term is pretty harmless. After all, there's nothing wrong with wanting to do something nice for another person, right? It can be fun to surprise your best friend with their favorite flowers on their birthday or watch your sister's kids so she and her husband can have a date night. All of these are kind and generous acts, but they don't necessarily make you a people pleaser.

Let's consider another scenario. Say you are walking through the mall, minding your own business and window shopping when someone who has their face in their phone walks out of a store and straight into you. Do you have the desire to apologize? Even though the scenario wasn't your fault? If you do, then you may be a people pleaser.

A people pleaser is a person who gets meaning and validation from other people. They will go out of their way to do tasks so they can be noticed and praised, often to the point where they will ignore their own needs and may even compromise their values and morals to fit in.

Difference Between People Pleasing and Generosity

There is a huge difference between being generous to other people and being a people pleaser. When you are being generous, you are doing certain acts with the goal of *both parties* sharing happiness and pleasure from the gesture. More often than not, you have a healthy view of who you are as a person and a well-balanced self-esteem.

If you are trying to people please, this comes from a place of low self-esteem and the need for the other person to give you approval and validation. You are doing the action because you want them to notice you and praise you or like you. In essence, you are making yourself subservient so that you will get approval.

It's possible that you will get what you want from the other person. They may notice your act, validate, and approve of what you did. However, more often than not, they will expect more. As a people pleaser, you will give it. You will also change who you are to please a vast array of people and fit in with various crowds.

Empaths and People Pleasing

Empaths aren't the only ones who can fall into the people-pleasing trap. Anyone who suffers from a lack of self-esteem or desires to fit in with a certain group can be affected by this condition. However, empaths fall into this role more often because of their relationships with toxic people, including narcissists. Because we have a kind and giving nature, others will break us down and mold us so that we are only able to serve them.

As a child, I had a friend who (looking back) had a lot of narcissistic traits. She was incredibly controlling, mean, and constantly broke me down with comments about how I looked and how I would never find a friend who was better than her. We had some fun times too, so being around her wasn't always unpleasant.

I had known this friend since kindergarten because we lived on the same street. As we got into junior high, this friend decided that she no longer wanted to hang out with me and that there were cooler people to be with. Since I had very few other friends (she would forbid me from hanging out with others or made it hard to talk to them), the thought of losing her was frightening and unbearable. To ensure that she didn't forget me, I went out of my way to do things that made her happy.

This included helping her do her chores (or just doing them for her while she talked on the phone), or hanging out with her other friends (whom I didn't like) and agreeing with whatever they said (even though I didn't). In the end, she still wound up dropping me. But this story has a happy ending. Once she was out of the picture, I had the freedom to hang out with other people and met some amazing friends that I still talk to today.

Most of the time, we don't know that others are manipulating us and breaking down our sense of self-worth. Thus, we begin to believe that to fit in with *everyone* around us, we have to bend over backward. Women are especially prone to becoming people pleasers because of societal pressures and values. They are always expected to put the needs of others first, especially their family's.

As an empath, when you are unable to distinguish between your emotions and another person's, this could be another reason why you feel like you need to make people happy. You are a natural fixer, and in your mind, the best way to fix things is to do tasks that need to be done—whether they are yours to do or not. You are also a natural peacemaker, so getting rid of conflict and keeping people happy is what you do.

Plus, as humans, we thrive in social situations. We don't want to be alone or an outcast. We want to spend time with people and have fun. When others view as different or weird because of our abilities, we may decide to mask them or act the way others do so we can be accepted.

Signs You Might Be a People Pleaser

It can be hard to know if the actions you take to be kind to others are generous or people-pleasing. Below are some questions to ask yourself to help you determine if you are people-pleasing or being generous.

1. **Do you pretend to agree with everyone?**

There's nothing wrong with listening politely to another person's opinion. This is a good social skill to have. However, if you don't agree with what they're saying or it goes against your values but you tell them that they are right so they'll like you, this is a people pleaser trait.

2. **Do you feel responsible for how others feel?**

Being an empath means that you often want to fix other people and make them feel better. However, if you find that you feel responsible for their emotions and that you have the power to make them happy, this could be a people pleaser sign. You can be there for another person, but they are ultimately responsible for their own emotions.

3. **How often do you apologize?**

If you apologize when you have done something wrong, and it's appropriate, this is a normal, healthy reaction. However, if you are constantly apologizing and are afraid that people are always blaming you for things, this could be a sign of a larger issue. You should apologize if something was your fault, but you shouldn't apologize for who you are.

4. **Do you feel burdened by the things you have to do?**

If you are a people pleaser, the vast majority of your day will be filled with doing things that other people want you to do—or that you *think* they want you to do. You will have very little time to do the things you want to do, and this could make you feel like you are burdened or stress you out because there isn't enough time in the day to get everything done.

Now, keep in mind that this doesn't apply to all situations. For example, there are chores and things you *have* to do at work or home that you may not want to do. Doing them doesn't necessarily make you a people pleaser. What would make you a people pleaser is if your ehaviour asks you to do *their* job and you agree because you don't want them to be mad at you or because you think they'll like you better.

5. Do you feel uncomfortable if someone is mad at you?

Even though you may be stressed and upset that you have too many things to do during the day, you will continue to do them because you can't stand it if someone is mad at you. In fact, you will more than likely go out of your way to try to make them happy with you again, even if that means compromising your values or morals.

6. Can you say no?

If you can't so no when someone asks you to do something, this could be another sign you have people pleaser tendencies.

Out of Control Empath

In addition to being a people pleaser, as an empath, you have the ability to lose control. This can happen for many reasons, including not knowing how to control the energy and emotions around you and exerting your thoughts and opinions onto others. Both of these can be detrimental to your well-being.

Before you reach the awareness stage of your empathic abilities, you may find that you constantly feel run down and exhausted. You may run yourself ragged trying to fix the world's problems and may not understand why you feel the way you do. This can lead to a lot of issues, including attracting and falling into the manipulations of toxic people or using substances to deal with or mask your feelings. If you also have people pleaser tendencies, you may be working overtime to make others like you and to fix their emotions.

The other part of being an out-of-control healer is knowing what you are capable of and using it to help others, even if they don't want your help. This can occur during the empowerment phase. While this is a good time for you to experiment and see how far you can take your abilities, forcing them on other people or intruding into their personal space isn't the best idea. It could lead to hurt feelings (yours and theirs) and the loss of trust and friendships.

Being able to pick up on another person's emotions is truly a gift. Yet, that doesn't mean you should use your skills in every situation. Just because you can read your ehaviour and realize that they are going through a tough time, they may not want to talk about it, especially when they are at work. They probably also don't want your unsolicited advice on how they should live their life.

Think of it this way: you are in a public place, say a train station or an airport, and you are with an acquaintance, someone you know but aren't super close with. They decide they have to go to the bathroom, so they ask if you will watch their luggage. You are more than happy to, and they get up to leave. While they are gone, you notice that their bag is open. You could easily dig through their bag and discover things about this person you didn't know, but this probably isn't the best idea. Imagine how they are going to react when they come back and see you doing this.

The same can be said about using your empathic abilities to delve into a person's emotional life. While you may not always be able to control or stop yourself from reading or absorbing their energy, you *do* have the ability to keep your mouth shut and not saying anything. You may decide to make a passing statement about being there if the other person needs to talk (but only if you want to), but don't take it beyond that. If they don't want you in their business, you need to stay out of it.

How These Pitfalls Impact You

When you engage in either people-pleasing or out-of-control empath behaviors, I have no doubt that your intentions are good. You want to use your ability to help others and make them feel better when they are going through a tough time. This is a noble gesture, but you need to make sure you aren't acting at the expense of your mental, emotional, and physical health.

If you constantly feel run down, exhausted, stressed, anxious, or even depressed, you are not putting yourself first. If others are always asking you to do things and you do them without question but then feel resentful or burdened by them, you aren't putting yourself first. You may also find yourself sharing your opinion or telling others how they should be living their life or how to fix a problem. This could lead to anger and resentment directed toward you. You may also find yourself looking for ways to numb yourself, possibly turning to drugs or alcohol, just so you don't have to deal with the emotions and energy swirling around you.

I'm sure I don't have to tell you that none of these behaviors are healthy and they will eventually take their toll. Before you get so rundown that you are sick or so deep into depression or addiction you don't know how to get out, you need to take some proactive steps and heal yourself.

Moving Beyond the Pitfalls

No one is perfect. As humans, we are all subject to a range of emotions and undesirable traits. This doesn't make us good or bad but a mixture of both. What we do with who we are will ultimately determine our worth. Empaths may have a tendency to be kinder and more caring than other individuals, but this isn't *always* the case. In addition, we aren't above falling into vices and other issues, including being a people pleaser or an out-of-control empath.

As always, the first step to moving beyond these pitfalls is recognizing that you are engaging in these behaviors. If you are uncertain or unsure if you are, then take a step back and take a long, hard look at your life. You'll need to do a gut check and really scrutinize how you feel. You can also ask those closest to you if they've noticed a change in your ehaviour. Listen to what they have to say, then look at it objectively and determine what needs to be fixed.

You may find that you can't do this on your own, and that's okay. Seek out the help of a close friend or family members or consider talking to a mental health professional. Being able to talk freely and openly about your fears, worries, and concerns is a great way to overcome them and make productive and lasting changes.

For your empathic abilities, you may search out others who share your gift. There are many communities online, including on Facebook, and there may be some in your local community. If there isn't, you might consider starting a group of your own.

Sometimes the best way to overcome a weakness and to develop strength is to be around people who are like you.

Some of the best ways to move beyond these pitfalls are the same methods we discussed earlier in this book. The biggest is to have healthy boundaries and relationship expectations. You should also put yourself first. This isn't selfish, and it doesn't mean that you have to take care of yourself at the expense of others. But you will have to determine what you want and need to be happy and healthy. If you don't take care of yourself, you can't expect to be able to take care of other people.

It's also important to be kind to yourself. If you realize that you've fallen into one of these pitfalls. Don't think that it makes you less of a human or a terrible empath. Again, no one is perfect. At least you are doing something to make a change. This says more about your strengths and abilities than anything else.

Chapter Summary

- Empaths are still humans, and they can fall into some pitfalls.

- Being kind and caring are great traits, but having low self-worth can lead to issues.

- Improving yourself and honing your skills can be viewed as a strength.

Final Words

MY GOAL WITH THIS BOOK was to give you an idea of what it's like being an empath and helping you figure out if you possess this amazing skill. Like anything in life, your journey as an empath will have its ups and downs, good times and bad. Some days you will enjoy your gift and revel in your ability to be closely connected to others and the universe, while others you will curse it for being able to feel as deeply as you do.

Throughout your journey, you will meet people who genuinely care for you and appreciate what you do for them, and you will also meet those who want to exploit and use you for their own ends. You'll have days when you are exhausted, anxious, maybe even depressed, but then there will be other days when you are floating on air.

No matter where you are currently in your journey, whether you are just having your awakening or you are at the empowerment stage, be good to yourself. If you aren't healthy and happy, it is a challenge to make other people healthy and happy.

Determine What's Best for You

You are the only one who can determine what is best for you. Even with your abilities to sense and absorb the energies and emotions of those around you, you're still in charge of your life. You're still the boss. People will try to pull you in many different directions and give you advice on what you should or shouldn't be doing, but you don't have to listen to them. Energy vampires, narcissists, and toxic people are really good at this, and they'll try to control every aspect of your life, but this isn't in your best interest. They're just looking for ways to get you to serve them.

Being in tune with energies and emotions means that you have the ability to sense other people's intentions. If you have a gut feeling about someone or they just don't seem to be right, trust it. No matter how broken or miserable or desperate another person seems, if it feels like something is wrong, there's a reason for that. Your "Spidey Sense" is tingling for a reason, and you need to listen to it.

In addition, don't be afraid or ashamed of your abilities. There's nothing wrong with being an empath and being able to connect to others and the world. If people try to make you feel different or weird because of your gift, then create some boundaries and decide how and when you want to interact with that person. They don't get to decide how you feel about being an empath, only you get to decide that.

Speaking of boundaries, they are essential to your empath journey and beyond. It's so easy to get caught up in others and the universe and lose yourself. When you take on other's emotions, you lose sight of which are yours and which are theirs. This is what will exhaust you and leave you feeling hollow. With boundaries, you give yourself the space you need to sort through your feelings and determine if they are really yours or someone else's. No matter what you find, whether they are yours or the world's, acknowledge them, fix what you can for yourself, and then let them go.

Take Time for You

One of the traits of an empath is the need to be alone to recharge. This is so important for your emotional, mental, and physical well-being. If you have a family with children, it can be hard to find time to get away. However, taking even 5 or 10 minutes each day may be all you need to recharge and de-stress. This is something you might consider doing first thing in the morning before everyone is awake or right before bed after you've got the kids settled in for the night. What you do during this downtime will depend on what you enjoy, but reading a book, meditating, or putting on some headphones and listening to music to block out the world can be beneficial.

Be a Good Listener

Your empathic skills already make you a good listener, which is why people come to you for advice and to share their news—both good and bad. Give yourself the same courtesy that you give others and listen to what your body is telling you. It's really good about letting you know when it's had enough and needs a break. Take one. This will ensure that you don't run yourself ragged and fall into an emotional state that's hard to get out of.

You also need to be kind to yourself. You give your friends, family, and perhaps even strangers your kindness and generosity because of your gifts, and you should do the same for yourself. Don't let anyone tell you that this is selfish because it's not. You can only give to others if you first give to yourself. Always remember that.

Have Fun!

Discovering who you are and honing your empathic skills shouldn't be a burden. Yes, there will be tough times and episodes where you are exhausted, stressed, and spent, but this is part of life. You can't always have sunshine and cloud-free days; storms roll in every once in a while. However, beneath the dark, foreboding, and menacing clouds is a bright, sunny sky. Things just need to clear for you to see it again. Nothing lasts forever, and the skies will eventually turn blue again.

When they do, don't forget to focus on the fun and enjoyable side of being an empath. Don't forget that you have an amazing and unique opportunity to be close to your friends and family, to understand them on a different level, and you should embrace that. Life is much too short to focus on the bad. Enjoy each moment and everyone who comes into your life. If they are negative and toxic, use it as a learning experience and move on.

Never Forget Who You Are

You are a kind, caring, and loving individual who has a unique opportunity to experience the world in ways that many people won't. You get to see how we are connected and be a part of something bigger than yourself. When you use this power to the best of your ability, you have the opportunity to change lives—including your own. Go forth and spread your kindness. The world can always use more.

If you enjoyed this book, remember to check out the companion books in the series, TOXIC MAGNETISM, about Empath's attraction to Narcissists, AM I CODEPENDENT, about an affliction that many empaths find themselves coping with, and INVSISIBLE ABUSE, about the covert abuse narcissists can deal out to empaths, sensitive people, and others. These books, along with the one you just read, are available on audio format as well.

Have you learned something or enjoyed reading? Please consider leaving a review! This is a big help to me in putting out more books like this one. Thank you, and good luck on your empathic journey!

www.ingramcontent.com/pod-product-compliance
Lightning Source LLC
Chambersburg PA
CBHW052100110526
44591CB00013B/2295